2002 SUPPLEMENT

CASES AND MATERIALS

FEDERAL COURTS

TENTH EDITION

by

CHARLES ALAN WRIGHT
Late Charles Alan Wright Chair in Federal Courts
The University of Texas

JOHN B. OAKLEY
Professor of Law, The University of California at Davis

NEW YORK, NEW YORK

FOUNDATION PRESS

2002

COPYRIGHT © 2000, 2001 FOUNDATION PRESS
COPYRIGHT © 2002 By FOUNDATION PRESS
                 395 Hudson Street
                 New York, NY 10014
                 Phone Toll Free 1–877–888–1330
                 Fax (212) 367–6799
                 fdpress.com

All rights reserved
Printed in the United States of America

ISBN 1–58778–358–4

 TEXT IS PRINTED ON 10% POST CONSUMER RECYCLED PAPER

PREFACE TO THE 2000 SUPPLEMENT

IN MEMORIAM
CHARLES ALAN WRIGHT
1927–2000

The extraordinary life of Charles Alan Wright ended, quite prematurely, on July 7, 2000. His illness was brief, and his death unexpected. This supplement, in press when he died, is no doubt only one of an array of posthumous publications. He wrote many volumes, and was always at work keeping each of them up to date. But this supplement and the casebook it accompanies were especially important to him. Professor Wright was above all a teacher, and the latest edition of the casebook was an essential part of his life, and of his legacy. He was 72 when he died, and his work on the casebook began when he was 33.

Our decision to publish a supplement was a close one. Expanding our annotations was not in itself a sufficient justification, but we concluded that the benefit to students of reading two new principal cases dealing with important aspects of removal law and habeas corpus justified the expense of a formal supplement rather than an informal, advisory message addressed only to instructors.

The occasion demands what words are ill-equipped to provide: an adequate testimonial to the stature of Professor Wright as an authority, a presence, a personality, a leader, and above all an exemplar in the teaching of the law of federal courts. My relationship to him originated with a letter that I wrote to him nearly twenty-five years ago, in my first year as a law teacher, questioning one statement made in a footnote on one page of the thousands of pages of his treatise on Federal Practice and Procedure. I was a novice. He was the dominant figure in his field. But he replied kindly, and at length. Students should bear this example in mind. Your views are important, and ultimately what matters is the merit of an argument, not the status of the proponent. We hope—and I write this collectively without any sense of contradiction—that you will be persuaded by reason rather than assertion that (where occasionally we may choose to reveal it) our view of the law of federal courts is correct.

JBO

Davis, California
July 10, 2000

*

PREFACE TO THE 2002 SUPPLEMENT

The Supreme Court's October 2001 Term proved to be a rich source of material for teaching Federal Courts. The 2002 Supplement features no fewer than 22 of these cases—six presented as new principal cases, and the other 16 referred to in supplementary commentary and annotations. This new material will allow instruction and discussion of many controversial doctrines to be organized around the freshest facts pondered by the Supreme Court, and to be illuminated by the Court's most recent teachings.

The first of the new principal cases is Raygor v. Regents of the University of Minnesota, 534 U.S. 533, 122 S.Ct. 999 (2002), added to Chapter II's material on supplemental jurisdiction. Its holding is narrow: to avoid constitutional doubt, the tolling provision of 28 U.S.C. § 1367(d) is somewhat artificially construed to be inapplicable to state-law claims asserted in federal court against a non-consenting state that have been dismissed on Eleventh Amendment grounds. It nonetheless merits inclusion as a principal case because it offers the Court's first overview of the history of § 1367, and because it touches on a wide range of divisive issues affecting federal jurisdiction: among others, the status and function of state sovereign immunity, the use of "clear statement" rules to reinforce state sovereign immunity even when Congress arguably has the power to overrule that immunity, and the discretionary nature of supplemental jurisdiction.

Raygor's emphasis on the need to construe strictly statutes in derogation of state sovereign immunity coheres nicely with the set of three new principal cases added to Chapter VIII's material on the Eleventh Amendment and related doctrines. The first of these is Federal Maritime Commission v. South Carolina State Ports Authority, 535 U.S. ___, 122 S.Ct. 1864 (2002), which continues the trend of recent 5-4 decisions extending the constitutional scope of state sovereign immunity substantially beyond the narrow limitation of Article III judicial power imposed by the literal text of the Eleventh Amendment. Here the "federalism five"—Chief Justice Rehnquist, Justice O'Connor, Justice Scalia, Justice Kennedy, and Justice Thomas— hold that a nonconsenting state cannot be made party to a federal administrative proceeding upon the complaint of a private party, and ground this holding on a perceived constitutional imperative to protect the "dignity" of state governments.

Federal Maritime Commission is followed by a refreshingly unanimous opinion, Lapides v. Board of Regents of the University System of Georgia, 535 U.S. ___, 122 S.Ct. 1640 (2002). Lapides breaks new ground in holding that state sovereign immunity can be waived by a state's litigation conduct even if the official responsible for the conduct in question—here, the state attorney general, who joined with individual defendants in removing the case from state to federal court—is not expressly authorized by state law to waive the state's Eleventh Amendment immunity.

The last of this new trilogy of Eleventh Amendment cases is Verizon Maryland Inc. v. Public Service Commission of Maryland, 536 U.S. ___, 122 S.Ct. 1753 (2002). After a subtle determination on complex facts that a state regulatory commission's construction of a federally authorized agreement between telecommunications carriers at least arguably arises under federal law, and hence may be reviewed by a federal district court in the exercise of its original jurisdiction under 28 U.S.C. § 1367, a unanimous eight-member Court (Justice O'Connor not participating) holds that Ex parte Young resoundingly trumps the state's objection to review of its commission's ruling in a federal district court.

Lee v. Kemna, 534 U.S. 362, 122 S.Ct. 877 (2002), is added to Chapter VIII's material on habeas corpus, but also applies directly to Chapter XI's discussion of the "adequacy" of an independent state ground asserted as a bar to direct appellate review of a state-court judgment. Chief Justice Rehnquist and Justice O'Connor join the six-Justice majority opinion rejecting the adequacy of the state's claim of procedural default. Justice Kennedy, joined in dissent by Justice Scalia and Justice Thomas, argues that the Court in effect revives the moribund precedent of Henry v. Mississippi, 379 U.S. 443 (1965), by engaging in circumstantial analysis of the inadequacy of the state's insistence that the defendant's federal due-process claim was waived for lack of procrustean compliance with state procedural law governing the making of a motion for a continuance.

Correctional Services Corporation v. Malesko, 534 U.S. 61, 122 S.Ct. 515 (2002), concludes the suite of new principal cases with a return to the familiar 5-4 juxtaposition of the "federalism five" in opposition to the Court's liberal wing of Justice Stevens, Justice Souter, Justice Ginsberg, and Justice Breyer. This case supplements Chapter IX's discussion of implied rights of action that have the effect of federalizing what would otherwise be claims redressable, if at all, solely as a matter of state law. The majority, obviously skeptical about the underpinnings of the line of cases founded on Bivens v. Six Unknown Federal Narcotics Agents, 403 U.S. 388 (1971), and continued by the main volume's principal case of Carlson v. Green, 446 U.S. 14 (1980), refuses to extend Bivens and Carlson to permit an incarcerated federal prisoner to bring a federal suit for damages against the private corporation that, as a federal contractor, was allegedly responsible for a serious infringement of the prisoner's Eighth Amendment rights.

Prominent among last Term's cases discussed in the annotations are Utah v. Evans, 536 U.S. ___, 122 S.Ct. 2191 (2002), which casts new light on the "redressability" requirement of Article III standing; Holmes Group, Inc. v. Vornado Air Circulation Systems, Inc., 535 U.S. ___, 122 S.Ct. 1889 (2002), which holds that the "well-pleaded complaint" rule bars grounding federal-question jurisdiction under 28 U.S.C. § 1331 on a federal counter-claim; Porter v. Nussle, 534 U.S. 516, 122 S.Ct. 983 (2002), which adopted a very broad construction of the requirement of exhaustion of state administrative remedies before a prisoner may bring suit under 42 U.S.C. § 1983; and Horn v. Banks, 536 U.S. ___, 122 S.Ct. 2147 (2002), holding that the bar on retrospective application of new rules of constitutional law articulated in Teague v. Lane, 489 U.S. 288 (1989), retains independent effect in the wake of AEDPA's subsequent curtailment of habeas relief.

The 2002 Supplement also includes numerous new references to important cases in the lower courts, some of which highlight circuit splits that the Supreme Court will resolve next Term, as well as academic commentary casting new light on perennial problems affecting the allocation of jurisdiction between state and federal courts.

JBO

Davis, California
July 3, 2002

*

TABLE OF CONTENTS

TABLE OF CASES

Principal cases are in bold type. Non-principal cases are in roman type. References are to Pages.

*

2002 SUPPLEMENT

CASES AND MATERIALS

FEDERAL COURTS

*

CHAPTER I

"JUDICIAL POWER" OVER "CASES AND CONTROVERSIES"

Page 13. Add to Footnote 5

The Court relaxed its view the next year, however. In Northern Pipeline Construction Co. v. Marathon Pipe Line Co., 458 U.S. 50, 88 (1982), discussed in the main volume at page 75, n. 47, the Court stayed the effect of a judgment holding unconstitutional certain jurisdictional provisions of the Bankruptcy Reform Act of 1978 in order to give Congress time to enact corrective legislation.

Page 13. Add to Footnote 6

The Third Circuit has disavowed its holding in Di Frischia on the ground that it cannot be reconciled with the Supreme Court's contrary holding in Owen Equipment & Erection Co. See Mennen Co. v. Atlantic Mut. Ins. Co., 147 F.3d 287, 294 n. 9 (3d Cir.1998).

Page 21. Add to Footnote 7

Any doubt that political cases do not necessarily present nonjusticiable "political questions" must be considered to have died with the Supreme Court's decision to review and decide issues determining the outcome of the 2000 Presidential election. Arguably the most remarkable aspect of the Court's two decisions in Bush v. Palm Beach County Canvassing Bd., 531 U.S. 70 (2000), and Bush v. Gore, 531 U.S. 98 (2000), is the failure in either opinion to mention the political-question doctrine, let alone to explain its inapplicability to a dispute over the process of appointment of state electors, a dispute that has arguably been committed by Article II and Amendment XII to resolution by the legislative branch rather than the judiciary. See Pushaw, *Bush v. Gore*: Looking at *Baker v. Carr* in a Conservative Mirror, 18 Const.Comm. 359 (2001); Pushaw, Judicial Review and the Political Question Doctrine: Reviving the Federalist "Rebuttable Presumption" Analysis, 80 N.C.L.Rev. 1165.

Page 26. Add to Footnote 11

Although no mention was made of the doctrine of third-party standing, the Court apparently relied upon it for its jurisdiction to decide Bush v. Gore, 531 U.S. 98 (2000). In that case the Court reversed a judgment of the Florida Supreme Court that it held violated the equal-protection rights not of petitioner Bush, but rather of Florida voters not party to the suit before it. See Pushaw, *Bush v. Gore*: Looking at *Baker v. Carr* in a Conservative Mirror, 18 Const. Comm. 359, 392 & n. 196 (2001).

Page 28. Add to Footnote 14

ASARCO is discussed in Elmendorf, Note, State Courts, Citizen Suits, and the Enforcement of Federal Environmental Law by Non–Article III Plaintiffs, 110 Yale L.J. 1003 (2001).

Page 30. Add to Footnote 15

In Friends of the Earth, Inc. v. Laidlaw Environmental Services (TOC), Inc., 528 U.S. 167 (2000), over the dissent of Justices Scalia and Thomas, the Court took an expansive view of the standing of environmental-protection organizations to seek to redress past violations of anti-pollution laws, and to deter future violations. The Court also clarified the relationship between the stringent initial requirement that plaintiffs have Article III standing and the more prudential and pragmatic analysis that governs whether a defendant's voluntary cessation of illegal conduct renders moot an otherwise justiciable claim to relief.

Page 49. Add to Footnote 28

In Vermont Agency of Natural Resources v. United States, 529 U.S. 765 (2000), discussed below in connection with p. 349, n. 14, and p. 418, n. 36, the Court held that a private party has standing to bring a qui tam suit on behalf of the United States under the False Claims Act.

A district court has the power and duty to oversee attorneys' fees paid to class counsel even if there is no common fund and class members are not directly affected by payments to counsel; supervision and control of fees paid to class counsel is an ancillary matter within the court's equitable jurisdiction whether or not an objecting class member has standing under Article III. Zucker v. Occidental Petroleum, 192 F.3d 1323 (9th Cir.1999).

Page 55.

In the twelfth line from the top of the page, insert new footnote 29a at the end of the citation to the Mottley case.

[29a. In the foregoing case, the Court dealt with a *prospective* legal challenge to the methodology of the 2000 census, i.e., one that was litigated before the census occurred. Thus the only serious issue of Article III standing confronting the Court in Clinton v. Glavin was whether the plaintiffs had suffered the requisite "personal injury"—not whether that injury was "fairly traceable" to the defendants' conduct or whether that injury was "likely to be redressed" by judicial relief.

In Utah v. Evans, 536 U.S. ___, 122 S.Ct. 2191 (2002), the Court dealt with a *retrospective* methodological challenge that Utah asserted in litigation commenced only after the census was completed, the results officially announced, and the House of Representatives accordingly reapportioned. Under the current statutes this reapportionment occurs automatically on the basis of the decennial census results that the President is required to transmit to the Congress no later than January 12 of the following year. Utah found itself with one fewer representative than it would have had if the Census Bureau had not used a methodology called "hot-deck imputation" to fill in gaps in the information that it had collected in 2000. North Carolina benefitted more from this methodology than did Utah, and thus gained a representative at Utah's expense. Despite the fact that there was no clear way to withdraw and revise the already-completed 2001 reapportionment (absent enactment of a new reapportionment statute) should Utah prevail in its federal suit challenging the Census Bureau's use of "hot-deck imputation," the Supreme Court held that it was unlikely that congressional and executive leaders would fail to find a way to correct an erroneous apportionment should the Court invalidate the use of "hot-deck imputation." Thus Utah's injury was sufficiently "likely to be redressed" by the only relief the Court directly could order—the issuance of corrected census figures by the Census Bureau—for Utah to have Article III standing. Only Justice Scalia dissented on standing grounds.]

Page 58. Add to Footnote 33

The requirement set forth in Aetna—that a declaratory-judgment case be one in which the controversy would admit "of specific relief through a decree of a conclusive character"—was not met where a condemned inmate sought a declaratory judgment as to which of two provisions of AEDPA (discussed at p. 495 et seq. of the main volume) would govern his as-yet unfiled habeas petition, and the suit was held nonjusticiable under Article III. Calderon v. Ashmus, 523 U.S. 740 (1998).

CHAPTER II

CASES ARISING UNDER THE CONSTITUTION AND LAWS OF THE UNITED STATES

Page 109.

In the sixth line from the top of the page, insert new footnote 11a at the end of the citation to the Mottley case.

[**11a.** The well-pleaded complaint rule bars basing statutory federal-question jurisdiction on a federal counterclaim, as well as on a federal defense, since a counterclaim, like a defense, is asserted in the answer rather than the complaint. See Holmes Group, Inc. v. Vornado Air Circulation Systems, Inc., 535 U.S. ___, 122 S.Ct. 1889 (2002), also discussed below in connection with p. 222, n. 16, and p. 750, n. 3.]

Page 136. Add to Footnote 28.

The Supreme Court has tended of late to cite to the tail rather than the head of the body of precedent created by Bell v. Hood and successor cases. The Court's currently favorite proxy is Steel Company v. Citizens for a Better Environment, 523 U.S. 83, 89 (1998), which in turn refers back to Bell v. Hood. One recent example of the continuing authority of Bell v. Hood, as carried forward by Steel Company, is Verizon Maryland Inc. v. Public Service Commission of Maryland, 536 U.S. ___, ___, 122 S.Ct. 1753, 1758–1759 (2002), reprinted below as a new principal case to be inserted at page 418 of the main volume. See infra, p. [___], at p. [___].

Another recent example may be found in Owasso Independent School District v. Falvo, 534 U.S. 426, ___, 122 S.Ct. 934, 938 (2002). This case raised issues of the scope of the Family Educational Rights and Privacy Act of 1974 (FERPA), 20 U.S.C. § 1232g. The issue of whether a private party harmed by a violation of FERPA may sue for relief under 42 U.S.C. § 1983 was pending before the Court in another, then undecided case. "Though we leave open the § 1983 question, the Court has subject-matter jurisdiction because respondent's federal claim is not so 'completely devoid of merit as not to involve a federal controversy.' Steel Co. v. Citizens for Better Environment, 523 U.S. 83, 89 (1998) (citation omitted). With these preliminary observations concluded, we turn to the merits." Four months later the Court decided that FERPA is *not* enforceable by a private suit under § 1983. See Gonzaga University v. Doe, 536 U.S. ___, 122 S.Ct. 2268 (2002), discussed below in connection with p. 627, n. 65, and p. 638, n. 70.

Page 154. Add to the carryover paragraph at the top of the page.

A suit to redress the breach of a settlement agreement that is within the ancillary jurisdiction recognized in Kokkonen may in exceptional circumstances be removed to federal court if it has been commenced in state court. Despite the lack of original jurisdiction, which precludes removal

4

under 28 U.S.C. § 1441(a), some courts have held removal authorized by some combination of ancillary jurisdiction and the All Writs Act. See, e.g., Montgomery v. Aetna Plywood, Inc., 231 F.3d 399, 411, n. 4 (7th Cir.2000) (collecting and analyzing conflicting authorities). As discussed below in connection with page 245, footnote 7, of the main volume, the Supreme Court has granted certiorari to resolve a circuit split on the district courts' power to remove cases under the All Writs Act.

Page 154. Add to the last paragraph of the Comments on § 1367.

Colloquy: Supplemental Jurisdiction, the ALI, and the Rule of *Kroger* Case, 51 Duke L.J. 647 (2001), consists of a four-part exchange between Professor Edward A. Hartnett and Professor Oakley. Continuing confusion among the circuit courts in the construction of § 1367 is documented and evaluated in Oakley, Joinder and Jurisdiction in the Federal District Courts: The State of the Union of Rules and Statutes, 69 Tenn. L.Rev. 35 (2001).

Page 154. Insert before Wasserman v. Potamkin Toyota, Inc.

Raygor v. Regents of the University of Minnesota

Supreme Court of the United States, 2002.
534 U.S. 533, 122 S.Ct. 999, 152 L.Ed.2d 27.

■ JUSTICE O'CONNOR delivered the opinion of the Court.

In federal court, petitioners asserted state law claims under the supplemental jurisdiction statute, 28 U.S.C. § 1367, against respondent university, an arm of the State of Minnesota. Those claims were dismissed on Eleventh Amendment grounds, and petitioners refiled them in state court past the period of limitations. The supplemental jurisdiction statute purports to toll the period of limitations for supplemental claims while they are pending in federal court and for 30 days after they are dismissed. § 1367(d). The Minnesota Supreme Court held that provision unconstitutional when applied to claims against nonconsenting state defendants, such as respondent university, and dismissed petitioners' claims. We affirm the judgment on the alternative ground that the tolling provision does not apply to claims filed in federal court against nonconsenting States.

I

In August 1995, petitioners Lance Raygor and James Goodchild filed charges with the Equal Employment Opportunity Commission (EEOC). The charges alleged that their employer, the University of Minnesota, discriminated against them on the basis of age in December 1994 by attempting to compel them to accept early retirement at the age of 52. After petitioners refused to retire, the university allegedly reclassified petitioners' jobs so as to reduce their salaries.

5

The EEOC cross-filed petitioners' charges with the Minnesota Department of Human Rights (MDHR) and later issued a right-to-sue letter on June 6, 1996, advising that petitioners could file a lawsuit within 90 days under the Age Discrimination in Employment Act of 1967 (ADEA), 81 Stat. 602, as amended, 29 U.S.C. § 621 et seq. The MDHR likewise issued right-to-sue letters on July 17, 1996, advising petitioners that they could file suit within 45 days under the Minnesota Human Rights Act (MHRA), Minn. Stat., ch. 363 (1991).

On or about August 29, 1996, each petitioner filed a separate complaint against respondent Board of Regents of the University of Minnesota (hereinafter respondent), in the United States District Court for the District of Minnesota. Each complaint alleged a federal cause of action under the ADEA and a state cause of action under the MHRA. The suits were subsequently consolidated. Respondent filed answers to these complaints in September 1996, setting forth eight affirmative defenses, including that the suits were " 'barred in whole or in part by Defendant's Eleventh Amendment immunity.' " . . .

In early July 1997, respondent filed its motion to dismiss petitioners' claims pursuant to Federal Rule of Civil Procedure 12(b)(1). The motion argued that the federal and state law claims were barred by the Eleventh Amendment. Petitioners' response acknowledged respondent's " 'potential Eleventh Amendment immunity from state discrimination claims in Federal Court,' " but urged the District Court to exercise supplemental jurisdiction over the state claims if the federal claims were upheld. On July 11, 1997, the District Court granted respondent's Rule 12(b)(1) motion and dismissed all of petitioners' claims. Petitioners appealed, but the appeal was stayed pending this Court's decision in Kimel v. Florida Bd. of Regents, 528 U.S. 62 (2000). *Kimel* held that the "ADEA does not validly abrogate the States' sovereign immunity." 528 U.S., at 92. Given that result, petitioners moved to withdraw their appeal, and it was dismissed in January 2000.

In the meantime, approximately three weeks after the Federal District Court had dismissed their state law claims, petitioners refiled their state law claims in Hennepin County District Court. Respondent's answer asserted that " 'plaintiff's claims are barred, in whole or in part, by the applicable statute of limitations.' " The state court initially stayed the lawsuit because of the pending federal appeal, but lifted the stay in December 1998 for the purpose of allowing respondent to move for dismissal on statute of limitations grounds. Respondent moved for summary judgment in February 1999, arguing that petitioners' state claims were barred by the applicable 45 day statute of limitations. See Minn.Stat. §§ 363.06, subd. 3, 363.14, subd. 1(a)(1) (2000). Respondent also argued that the tolling provision of the federal supplemental jurisdiction statute, 28 U.S.C. § 1367, did not apply to toll the limitations period on the state law claims while they were pending in federal court because the Federal District Court never had subject matter jurisdiction over petitioners' ADEA claims. Petitioners argued that the tolling provision of the supplemental jurisdiction statute applied because their state law claims had been dismissed without prejudice. The State District Court treated respondent's motion for summary judgment as a motion to dismiss and granted it, holding that § 1367(d) did "not apply ... because the federal district court never had 'original jurisdiction' over the controversy" since "both the state and federal claims were dismissed for lack of subject matter jurisdiction."

The Minnesota Court of Appeals reversed. The court first decided that the Federal District Court had original jurisdiction over the case before respondent's Eleventh Amendment defense was "successfully asserted." 604 N.W.2d [128], at 132 [(Min.App. 2000)] (citing Wisconsin Dept. of Corrections v. Schacht, 524 U.S. 381 (1998)). The court then held that § 1367(d) applied to toll the statute of limitations for petitioners' state law claims because that provision "allows tolling of any claim dismissed by a federal district court, whether dismissed on Eleventh Amendment grounds or at the discretion of the federal district court under [§ 1367](c)." 604 N.W.2d, at 132–133 .

The Minnesota Supreme Court reversed. The court noted that respondent was an arm of the State, and found that the federal tolling provision facially applied to petitioners' state law claims. 620 N.W.2d [680], at 684, 687 [(Min. 2001)]. The court concluded, however, "that application of section 1367(d) to toll the statute of limitations applicable to state law claims against an unconsenting state defendant first filed in federal court but then dismissed and brought in state court is an impermissible denigration of [respondent's] Eleventh Amendment immunity." Id., at 687. The court thus concluded that § 1367(d) could not constitutionally apply to toll the statute of limitations for petitioners' state law claims, and it dismissed those claims. We granted certiorari, 532 U.S. 1065 (2001), on the question whether 28 U.S.C. § 1367(d) is unconstitutional as applied to a state defendant.

II

In Mine Workers v. Gibbs, 383 U.S. 715 (1966), this Court held that federal courts deciding claims within their federal-question subject matter jurisdiction, 28 U.S.C. § 1331, may decide state law claims not within their subject matter jurisdiction if the federal and state law claims "derive from a common nucleus of operative fact" and comprise "but one constitutional 'case.'" *Mine Workers*, supra, at 725. Jurisdiction over state law claims in such instances was known as "pendent jurisdiction." This Court later made clear that absent authorization from Congress, a district court could not exercise pendent jurisdiction over claims involving parties who were not already parties to a claim independently within the court's subject matter jurisdiction. See Finley v. United States, 490 U.S. 545 (1989).

In the wake of *Finley*, the Federal Courts Study Committee recommended that "Congress expressly authorize federal courts to hear any claim arising out of the same 'transaction or occurrence' as a claim within federal jurisdiction, including claims, within federal question jurisdiction, that require the joinder of additional parties." Report of Federal Courts Study Committee 47 (Apr. 2, 1990). Soon thereafter, Congress enacted the supplemental jurisdiction statute, 28 U.S.C. § 1367, as part of the Judicial Improvements Act of 1990. Subsection (a) of § 1367 states that

"[e]xcept as provided in subsections (b) and (c) or as expressly provided otherwise by Federal statute, in any civil action of which the district courts have original jurisdiction, the district courts shall have supplemental jurisdiction over all other claims that are so related to claims in the action within such original jurisdiction that they form part of the same case or controversy under Article III of the United States Constitution. Such supplemental jurisdiction shall include claims that involve the joinder or intervention of additional parties."

Subsection (b) places limits on supplemental jurisdiction when the district court's original jurisdiction is based only on diversity of citizenship jurisdiction under 28 U.S.C. § 1332. Subsection (c) allows district courts to decline to exercise supplemental jurisdiction in certain situations, such as when a "claim raises a novel or complex issue of State law." § 1367(c)(1).

Petitioners originally sought to have their state law claims heard in federal court as supplemental claims falling under § 1367(a). Prior to the enactment of § 1367, however, this Court held that the Eleventh Amendment bars the adjudication of pendent state law claims against nonconsenting state defendants in federal court. See Pennhurst State School and Hospital v. Halderman, 465 U.S. 89, 120 (1984). In that context, the Eleventh Amendment was found to be an "explicit limitation on federal jurisdiction." Id., at 118. Consequently, an express grant of jurisdiction over such claims would be an abrogation of the sovereign immunity guaranteed by the Eleventh Amendment. Before Congress could attempt to do that, it must make its intention to abrogate " 'unmistakably clear in the language of the statute.' " Dellmuth v. Muth, 491 U.S. 223, 228 (1989) (quoting Atascadero State Hospital v. Scanlon, 473 U.S. 234, 242 (1985)).

The most that can be said about subsection (a), however, is that it is a general grant of jurisdiction, no more specific to claims against nonconsenting States than the one at issue in Blatchford v. Native Village of Noatak, 501 U.S. 775 (1991). There, we considered whether 28 U.S.C. § 1362 contained a clear statement of an intent to abrogate state sovereign immunity. That grant of jurisdiction provides that

"[t]he district courts shall have original jurisdiction of *all civil actions,* brought by any Indian tribe or band with a governing body duly recognized by the Secretary of the Interior, wherein the matter in controversy arises under the Constitution, laws, or treaties of the United States." (Emphasis added.)

Such a facially broad grant of jurisdiction over "all civil actions" could be read to include claims by Indian tribes against nonconsenting States, but we held that such language was insufficient to constitute a clear statement of an intent to abrogate state sovereign immunity. *Blatchford,* supra, at 786. Likewise, we cannot read § 1367(a) to authorize district courts to exercise jurisdiction over claims against nonconsenting States, even though nothing in the statute expressly excludes such claims. Thus, consistent with *Blatchford,* we hold that § 1367(a)'s grant of jurisdiction does not extend to claims against nonconsenting state defendants.

Even so, there remains the question whether § 1367(d) tolls the statute of limitations for claims against nonconsenting States that are asserted under § 1367(a) but subsequently dismissed on Eleventh Amendment grounds. Subsection (d) of § 1367 provides that

"[t]he period of limitations for any claim asserted under subsection (a), and for any other claim in the same action that is voluntarily dismissed at the same time as or after the dismissal of the claim under subsection (a), shall be tolled while the claim is pending and for a period of 30 days after it is dismissed unless State law provides for a longer tolling period."

On its face, subsection (d) purports to apply to dismissals of "*any* claim asserted under subsection (a)." Ibid. (emphasis added). Thus, it could be broadly read to apply to any claim technically "asserted" under subsection (a) as long as it was later dismissed, regardless of the reason for dismissal. But reading subsection (d) to apply when state law claims against nonconsenting States are dismissed on Eleventh Amendment grounds raises serious doubts about the constitutionality of the provision given principles of state sovereign immunity. If subsection (d) applied in such circumstances, it would toll the state statute of limitations for 30 days in addition to however long the claim had been pending in federal court. This would require a State to defend against a claim in state court that had never been filed in state court until some indeterminate time after the original limitations period had elapsed.

When the sovereign at issue is the United States, we have recognized that a limitations period may be "a central condition" of the sovereign's waiver of immunity. United States v. Mottaz, 476 U.S. 834, 843 (1986); see also Block v. North Dakota ex rel. Board of Univ. and School Lands, 461 U.S. 273, 287 (1983) ("When waiver legislation contains a statute of limitations, the limitations provision constitutes a condition on the waiver of sovereign immunity"). In suits against the United States, however, there is a rebuttable presumption that equitable tolling under federal law applies to waivers of the United States' immunity. See Irwin v. Department of Veterans Affairs, 498 U.S. 89, 95 (1990). From this, the dissent argues that any broadening of a State's waiver of immunity through tolling under § 1367(d) presumptively does not violate the State's sovereign immunity.... But this Court has never held that waivers of a State's immunity

9

presumptively include all federal tolling rules, nor is it obvious that such a presumption would be "a realistic assessment of legislative intent." *Irwin,* supra, at 95.

Moreover, with respect to suits against a state sovereign in its own courts, we have explained that a State "may prescribe the terms and conditions on which it consents to be sued," Beers v. Arkansas, 20 How. [61 U.S.] 527, 529 (1858), and that "[o]nly the sovereign's own consent could qualify the absolute character of [its] immunity" from suit in its own courts, Nevada v. Hall, 440 U.S. 410, 414 (1979). Thus, although we have not directly addressed whether federal tolling of a state statute of limitations constitutes an abrogation of state sovereign immunity with respect to claims against state defendants, we can say that the notion at least raises a serious constitutional doubt.

Consequently, we have good reason to rely on a clear statement principle of statutory construction. When "Congress intends to alter the 'usual constitutional balance between the States and the Federal Government,' it must make its intention to do so 'unmistakably clear in the language of the statute.' " Will v. Michigan Dept. of State Police, 491 U.S. 58, 65 (1989) (quoting *Atascadero,* supra, at 242). This principle applies when Congress "intends to pre-empt the historic powers of the States" or when it legislates in " 'traditionally sensitive areas' " that " 'affec[t] the federal balance.' " *Will,* supra, at 65 (quoting United States v. Bass, 404 U.S. 336, 349 (1971)). In such cases, the clear statement principle reflects "an acknowledgment that the States retain substantial sovereign powers under our constitutional scheme, powers with which Congress does not readily interfere." Gregory v. Ashcroft, 501 U.S. 452, 461, 464 (1991).

Here, allowing federal law to extend the time period in which a state sovereign is amenable to suit in its own courts at least affects the federal balance in an area that has been a historic power of the States, whether or not it constitutes an abrogation of state sovereign immunity. Thus, applying the clear statement principle helps " 'assur[e] that the legislature has in fact faced, and intended to bring into issue, the critical matters involved in the judicial decision.' " *Will,* supra, at 65 (quoting *Bass,* supra, at 349). This is obviously important when the underlying issue raises a serious constitutional doubt or problem. See Vermont Agency of Natural Resources v. United States ex rel. Stevens, 529 U.S. 765, 787 (2000) (relying in part on clear statement principle to decide the False Claims Act, 31 U.S.C. §§ 3729–3733, did not authorize "an action in federal court by a qui tam relator against a State" and avoiding whether such a suit would violate the Eleventh Amendment, an issue raising a serious constitutional doubt); *Gregory,* supra, at 464 (relying on clear statement principle to determine that state judges were excluded from the ADEA in order to "avoid a potential constitutional problem" given the constraints on the Court's "ability to consider the limits that the state-federal balance places on Congress' powers under the Commerce Clause").

The question then is whether § 1367(d) states a clear intent to toll the limitations period for claims against nonconsenting States that are dismissed on Eleventh Amendment grounds. Here the lack of clarity is apparent in two respects. With respect to the *claims* the tolling provision covers, one could read § 1367(d) to cover any claim "asserted" under subsection (a), but we have previously found similarly general language insufficient to satisfy clear statement requirements. For example, we have held that a statute providing civil remedies for violations committed by " *'any* recipient of Federal assistance' " was "not the kind of unequivocal statutory language sufficient to abrogate the Eleventh Amendment" even when it was undisputed that a State defendant was a recipient of federal aid. *Atascadero*, 473 U.S., at 245–246 (quoting 29 U.S.C. § 794a(a)(2) (1982 ed.) (emphasis in original)). Instead, we held that "[w]hen Congress chooses to subject the States to federal jurisdiction, it must do so specifically." 473 U.S., at 246. Likewise, § 1367(d) reflects no specific or unequivocal intent to toll the statute of limitations for claims asserted against nonconsenting States, especially considering that such claims do not fall within the proper scope of § 1367(a) as explained above.

With respect to the *dismissals* the tolling provision covers, one could read § 1367(d) in isolation to authorize tolling regardless of the reason for dismissal, but § 1367(d) occurs in the context of a statute that specifically contemplates only a few grounds for dismissal. The requirements of § 1367(a) make clear that a claim will be subject to dismissal if it fails to "form part of the same case or controversy" as a claim within the district court's original jurisdiction. Likewise, § 1367(b) entails that certain claims will be subject to dismissal if exercising jurisdiction over them would be "inconsistent" with 28 U.S.C. § 1332. Finally, § 1367(c) lists four specific situations in which a district court may decline to exercise supplemental jurisdiction over a particular claim. Given that particular context, it is unclear if the tolling provision was meant to apply to dismissals for reasons unmentioned by the statute, such as dismissals on Eleventh Amendment grounds. See Davis v. Michigan Dept. of Treasury, 489 U.S. 803, 809 (1989) ("It is a fundamental canon of statutory construction that the words of a statute must be read in their context and with a view to their place in the overall statutory scheme"). In sum, although § 1367(d) may not clearly exclude tolling for claims against nonconsenting States dismissed on Eleventh Amendment grounds, we are looking for a clear statement of what the rule *includes*, not a clear statement of what it *excludes*. See *Gregory*, 501 U.S., at 467. Section 1367(d) fails this test. As such, we will not read § 1367(d) to apply to dismissals of claims against nonconsenting States dismissed on Eleventh Amendment grounds.

In anticipation of this result, petitioners argue that the tolling provision should be interpreted to apply to their claims because Congress enacted it to prevent due process violations caused by state claim preclusion and anti-claim-splitting laws. In other words, petitioners contend that Congress enacted the tolling provision to enforce the Due Process Clause of the Fourteenth Amendment against perceived state violations. We have previously addressed the argument that if a statute were passed pursuant to Congress' § 5 powers under the Fourteenth Amendment, federalism concerns "might carry less weight." *Gregory,* 501 U.S., at 468. We concluded, however, that "the Fourteenth Amendment does not override all principles of federalism," id., at 469, and held that insofar as statutory intent was ambiguous, we would not "not attribute to Congress an intent to intrude on state governmental functions regardless of whether Congress acted pursuant to ... § 5 of the Fourteenth Amendment." Id., at 470. That same rule applies here. As already demonstrated, it is far from clear whether Congress intended tolling to apply when claims against nonconsenting States were dismissed on Eleventh Amendment grounds. Thus, it is not relevant whether Congress acted pursuant to § 5.

Petitioners also argue that our construction of the statute does not resolve their case because respondent consented to suit in federal court. We have stated that "[a] sovereign's immunity may be waived" and have "held that a State may consent to suit against it in federal court." *Pennhurst,* 465 U.S., at 99 (citing Clark v. Barnard, 108 U.S. 436, 447 (1883)). Petitioners claim that respondent consented to suit by not moving to dismiss petitioners' state law claims on Eleventh Amendment grounds until July 1997, some 10 months after the federal lawsuits were filed in August 1996. Yet respondent raised its Eleventh Amendment defense at the earliest possible opportunity by including that defense in its answers that were filed in September 1996. Given that, we cannot say that respondent "unequivocally expressed" a consent to be sued in federal court. *Pennhurst,* supra, at 99 (citing Edelman v. Jordan, 415 U.S. 651, 673 (1974)). The fact that respondent filed its motion in July 1997 is as consistent with adherence to the pretrial schedule as it is with anything else.

Indeed, such circumstances are readily distinguishable from the limited situations where this Court has found a State consented to suit, such as when a State voluntarily invoked federal court jurisdiction or otherwise "ma[de] a 'clear declaration' that it intends to submit itself to our jurisdiction." College Savings Bank v. Florida Prepaid Postsecondary Ed. Expense Bd., 527 U.S. 666, 676 (1999). And even if we were to assume for the sake of argument that consent could be inferred "from the failure to raise the objection at the outset of the proceedings," Wisconsin Dept. of Corrections v. Schacht, 524 U.S., at 395 (KENNEDY, J., concurring)—a standard this Court has not adopted[1]—consent would still not be found here since respondent raised the issue in its answer. Thus, we find no merit to petitioners' argument that respondent was a consenting state defendant

---

1. [In Lapides v. Board of Regents of the University System of Georgia, 535 U.S. ___, 122 S.Ct. 1640 (2002), reprinted below as a principal case following page 418 of the main volume, a unanimous Court later adopted the core principle of Justice Kennedy's concurrence in Schacht by holding that a state's litigation conduct may indeed constitute an implied waiver of its Eleventh Amendment immunity.]

during the federal court proceedings. We express no view on the application or constitutionality of § 1367(d) when a State consents to suit or when a defendant is not a State.

III

We hold that respondent never consented to suit in federal court on petitioners' state law claims and that § 1367(d) does not toll the period of limitations for state law claims asserted against nonconsenting state defendants that are dismissed on Eleventh Amendment grounds. Therefore, § 1367(d) did not operate to toll the period of limitations for petitioners' claims, and we affirm the judgment of the Minnesota Supreme Court dismissing those claims.

It is so ordered.

■ JUSTICE GINSBURG, concurring in part and concurring in the judgment.

I join the Court's judgment and its opinion in principal part. I agree with the decision's twin rulings. First, prevailing precedent supports the view that, in the absence of a clear statement of congressional intent to abrogate the States' Eleventh Amendment immunity, 28 U.S.C. § 1367(a)'s extension of federal jurisdiction does not reach claims against nonconsenting state defendants. Second, absent "affirmative indicatio[n]" by Congress, see Vermont Agency of Natural Resources v. United States ex rel. Stevens, 529 U.S. 765, 787 (2000), § 1367(d)'s tolling provision does not reach claims "asserted," but not maintainable, under § 1367(a) against nonconsenting state defendants.

The pathmarking decision, it appears to me, is *Vermont Agency.*[2] There, the Court declined to read the word "person," for purposes of qui tam liability, to include a nonconsenting State. Bolstering the Court's conclusion in *Vermont Agency* were the two reinforcements pivotal here: first, " 'the ordinary rule of statutory construction' that 'if Congress intends to alter the usual constitutional balance between States and the Federal Government, it must make its intention to do so un 6–A mistakably clear in the language of the statute,' " 529 U.S., at 787 (quoting Will v. Michigan Dept. of State Police, 491 U.S. 58, 65 (1989)); and second, "the doctrine that statutes should be construed so as to avoid difficult constitutional questions," 529 U.S., at 787. I would not venture further into the mist surrounding § 1367 to inquire, generally, whether § 1367(d) "appl[ies] to dismissals for reasons unmentioned by the statute," ante, at [11].[3]

---

2. This Court's majority, in contrast to the Minnesota Supreme Court, does not invoke Alden v. Maine, 527 U.S. 706 (1999), in support of today's decision. I joined the dissent in *Alden* and, in a suitable case, would join a call to reexamine that decision. . . .

3. The supplemental jurisdiction statute, well-reasoned commentary indicates, "is clearly flawed and needs repair." Oakley, Prospectus for the American Law Institute's Federal Judicial Code Revision Project, 31 U.C.D.L.Rev. 855, 936 (1998); see

■ JUSTICE STEVENS, with whom JUSTICE SOUTER and JUSTICE BREYER join, dissenting.

The federal interest in the fair and efficient administration of justice is both legitimate and important. To vindicate that interest federal rulemakers and judges have occasionally imposed burdens on the States and their judiciaries. Thus, for example, Congress may provide for the adjudication of federal claims in state courts, Testa v. Katt, 330 U.S. 386 (1947), and may direct that state litigation be stayed during the pendency of bankruptcy proceedings, 11 U.S.C. § 362(a). In appropriate cases federal judges may enjoin the prosecution of state judicial proceedings. By virtue of the Supremacy Clause in Article VI of the Constitution, in all such cases the federal rules prevail "and the Judges in every State shall be bound thereby, any Thing in the Constitution or Laws of any State to the Contrary notwithstanding."

The "supplemental jurisdiction" provisions of the Judicial Improvements Act of 1990, 28 U.S.C. § 1367, impose a lesser burden on the States than each of these examples, and do so only in a relatively narrow category of cases—those in which both federal-and state-law claims are so related "that they form part of the same case or controversy." Adopting a recommendation of the Federal Courts Committee, Congress in § 1367(a) overruled our misguided decision in Finley v. United States, 490 U.S. 545 (1989), and expressly authorized federal courts to entertain such cases even when the state-law claim is against a party over whom there is no independent basis for federal jurisdiction.

Subsection (d) of § 1367 responds to the risk that the plaintiff's state-law claim, even though timely when filed as a part of the federal lawsuit, may be dismissed after the state period of limitations has expired. To avoid the necessity of duplicate filings, it provides that the state statute shall be tolled while the claim is pending in federal court and for 30 days thereafter. The impact of this provision on the defendant is minimal, because the timely filing in federal court provides it with the same notice as if a duplicate complaint had also been filed in state court.

The tolling of statutes of limitations is, of course, an ancient[4] and

generally id., at 936–945 (canvassing problems with 28 U.S.C. § 1367). For a proposed repair of § 1367, see ALI, Federal Judicial Code Revision Project (Tent. Draft No. 2, Apr. 14, 1998).

4. When an equity bill was dismissed to permit the commencement of an action at law, it was the practice of the English courts to consider the statute of limitations tolled during the pendency of the suit in equity. See, e.g., Anonimous, 1 Vern. 73, 73–74, 23 Eng. Rep. 320, 320–321 (Ch. 1682) ("[I]f a man sued in Chancery, and pending the suit here, the statute of limitations attached on his demand, and his bill was afterwards dismissed, as being a matter properly determinable at common law: in such case ... [the court] would not suffer the statute to be pleaded in bar to his demand"); see also Sturt v. Mellish, 2 Atk. 610, 615, 26 Eng. Rep. 765, 767 (Ch. 1743); MacKenzie v. Marquis of Powis, 7 Brown 282, 288, 3 Eng. Rep. 183, 187 (H.L. 1737).

widespread practice.[5] Some federal tolling statutes apply only to federal limitations periods, but others apply to state statutes as well. All of these statutes are broadly worded and none of them excludes any special category of defendants. The plain text of all these statutes, including § 1367, applies to cases in which a State, or an arm of a State, is named as a defendant. Thus, as the Minnesota Court of Appeals correctly held, "the plain language of subsection (d) allows tolling of any claim dismissed by a federal district court, whether dismissed on Eleventh Amendment grounds or at the discretion of the federal district court under subsection (c)."[6]

The Minnesota Supreme Court reversed, because it considered this Court's holding in Alden v. Maine, 527 U.S. 706 (1999), to compel the view that § 1367(d) was an invalid attempt by Congress to make the State of Minnesota subject to suit in state court without its consent. Unlike the State in *Alden,* however, Minnesota has given its consent to be sued in its own courts for alleged violations of the MHRA within 45 days of receipt of a notice letter from the State Department of Human Rights. The question whether that timeliness condition may be tolled during the pendency of an action filed in federal court within the 45–day period is quite different from the question whether Congress can entirely abrogate the State's sovereign immunity defense. For the Court's Eleventh Amendment jurisprudence concerns the question *whether* an unconsenting sovereign may be sued, rather than *when* a consenting sovereign may be sued.

. . . . .

It is true, of course, that the federal tolling provision, like any other federal statute that pre-empts state law, "affects the federal balance" even though it does not "constitut[e] an abrogation of state sovereign immunity." Ante, at [10]. But that consequence is surely not sufficient to exclude state parties from the coverage of statutes of general applicability like the Bankruptcy Code, the Soldiers' and Sailors' Civil Relief Act of 1940, or any other federal statute whose general language creates a conflict with a pre-existing rule of state law. In my judgment, the specific holding in Alden v. Maine represented a serious distortion of the federal balance intended by the Framers of our Constitution. If that case is now to provide the basis for a rule of construction that will exempt state parties from the coverage of

---

5. Equitable tolling is a background rule that informs our construction of federal statutes of limitations, Holmberg v. Armbrecht, 327 U.S. 392, 397 (1946), including those statutes conditioning the Federal Government's waiver of immunity to suit, Irwin v. Department of Veterans Affairs, 498 U.S. 89, 95–96 (1990) ("[T]he same rebuttable presumption of equitable tolling applicable to suits against private defen-

dants should also apply to suits against the United States"). The rule also is generally applied by state courts, such as the Minnesota courts adjudicating claims under the Minnesota Human Rights Act (MHRA). See, e.g., Ochs v. Streater, Inc., 568 N.W.2d 858, 860 (Minn.App.1997).

6. 604 N.W.2d 128, 132–133 (Minn.App. 2000).

federal statutes of general applicability, whether or not abrogation of Eleventh Amendment immunity is at stake, it will foster unintended and unjust consequences and impose serious burdens on an already-overworked Congress. Indeed, that risk provides an additional reason for reexamining that misguided decision at the earliest opportunity.

Accordingly, I respectfully dissent.

CHAPTER III

DIVERSITY OF CITIZENSHIP

Page 158. Add to Footnote 2

Taking a narrow view of the domestic-relations exception, the Eleventh Circuit has held that a wife's fraudulent diversion of certain assets of her disabled husband—discovered but not pursued during the divorce proceedings, even though the diversion could have been asserted as grounds for increasing alimony—could be adjudicated by a federal court in a diversity action brought by the disabled husband's guardian against the former wife after the divorce proceedings had been completed. Dunn v. Cometa, 238 F.3d 38 (1st Cir. 2001).

Page 158. Add to Footnote 5

JPMorgan Chase Bank v. Traffic Stream (BVI) Infrastructure Limited, 536 U.S. ___, 122 S.Ct. 2054 (2002), provides a helpful overview of the history of and justification for federal alienage jurisdiction. A unanimous Court held that a corporation organized under the laws of the British Virgin Islands, a dependency of the United Kingdom, was a "citize[n] or subjec[t] of a foreign state" for purposes of 28 U.S.C. § 1332(a)(2).

Page 159. Add to Footnote 7

The circuits are divided with regard to the foreign-sovereign status of a corporation, a majority of whose shares are owned by holding company majority-owned by a foreign state. The Seventh Circuit has held that such a corporation is a foreign state under the FSIA; the Ninth Circuit has held to the contrary. See Alejandre v. Telefonica Larga Distancia de Puerto Rico, Inc., 183 F.3d 1277 (11th Cir.1999), in which the Eleventh Circuit discusses the conflicting cases but does not align itself with either position.

Page 160. Add to Footnote 9

The "older, and sounder" view endorsed by the main volume, that a national bank is "located" only in the state in which the bank has its principal place of business, was upheld by Judge Yohn in his comprehensive and erudite opinion in Financial Software Systems, Inc. v. First Union National Bank, 84 F.Supp.2d 594 (E.D.Pa. 1999).

Page 181. Add to Footnote 20

Note that Freeport–McMoRan, Inc. v. K N Energy, Inc., 498 U.S. 426 (1991), discussed in the second paragraph of this footnote as printed in the main volume, was decided three months before the new supplemental-jurisdiction, 28 U.S.C. § 1367, took effect. It appears to rely on the old rule extending ancillary jurisdiction to claims by or against nondiverse intervenors who were not "indispensable" parties. The new statute forbids supplemental jurisdiction over claims by intervening plaintiffs "when exercising supplemental jurisdiction over such claims would be inconsistent with the jurisdictional requirements of section 1332"—which presumably include the rule of complete diversity. The result reached in Freeport–McMoRan can be sustained, however, by characterizing the joinder of the newly added, nondiverse party as the *substitution* of a new party under Rule 25 of the Federal Rules of Civil Procedure, rather than as the *intervention* of that party under Rule 24. Rule 25(c) permits a new party which has succeeded to the interests of an existing party to be joined without requiring the dropping of the existing party from the litigation. Section 1367(b) imposes no limitation on the exercise of supplemental jurisdiction with respect to a new party joined under Rule 25. Compare the status of supplemental jurisdiction with respect to parties joinder under Rule 23, which is discussed at length in the Meritcare case at p. 231 of the main volume.

CHAPTER IV

JURISDICTIONAL AMOUNT

Page 209. Add to Footnote 2

See Note, Pleading to Stay in State Court: Forum Control, Federal Removal Jurisdiction, and the Amount in Controversy Requirement, 56 Wash. & Lee L.Rev. 651 (1999).

Page 219. Add to Footnote 15

The Supreme Court has granted certiorari in a case in which the Ninth Circuit reaffirmed the rule of Snow v. Ford Motor Co., again holding that the jurisdictional-amount requirement for removal of a consumer class action between diverse parties cannot be trumped by looking to the large cost to the defendants of complying with a requested injunction rather than the slight value of the benefit that the injunction would confer on each member of the plaintiff class. See In re Ford Motor Company/Citibank (South Dakota), N.A., 264 F.3d 952 (9th Cir.2001), cert. granted sub nom. Ford Motor Co. v. McCauley, ___ U.S. ___, 122 S.Ct. 1063 (2002).

Page 222. Add to Footnote 16

In the related context of statutory federal-question rather than diversity jurisdiction, the Supreme Court has recently made clear that counterclaims are irrelevant for purposes to determining whether a case "arises under" federal law. See Holmes Group, Inc. v. Vornado Air Circulation Systems, Inc., 535 U.S. ___, 122 S.Ct. 1889 (2002), also discussed above in connection with p. 109, n. 11a, and below in connection p. 750, n. 3.

Page 238. Add to Footnote 26

Hopes for a resolution of the conflict between the circuits described in the Meritcare case were dashed when the Fifth Circuit's jurisdictional decision in the Abbott Laboratories case was affirmed by an equally divided Court, Justice O'Connor not participating. Free v. Abbott Laboratories, Inc., 529 U.S. 333 (2000).

CHAPTER V

REMOVAL JURISDICTION AND PROCEDURE

Page 242. Add to Footnote 1

As discussed above in connection with page 154 of the main volume, some circuits have held that in exceptional circumstances a case not within the original jurisdiction of the district courts may be removed on the authority of the All Writs Act.

Page 242. Add to Footnote 2

The Violence Against Women Act (VAWA) was held unconstitutional in United States v. Morrison, 529 U.S. 598 (2000). This renders superfluous the prohibition on removal of VAWA claims enacted by VAWA as 28 U.S.C. § 1445(d).

Page 245. Add to Footnote 7

There are many specialized removal provisions enacted outside of Title 28 of the U.S. Code. In general they expand rather than restrict the right of removal provided by the general removal statutes, 28 U.S.C. §§ 1441–1447. See, e.g., the Securities Litigation Uniform Standards Act of 1998, discussed below in connection with p. 703, n. 45. See also Hoffman, Removal Jurisdiction and the All Writs Act, 148 U.Pa.L.Rev. 401 (1999); Steinman, The Newest Frontier of Judicial Activism: Removal Under the All Writs Act, 80 Bos.Univ.L.Rev. 773 (2000).

Aligning itself with the Ninth and Tenth Circuits, and rejecting the contrary view of the Second, Sixth, and Eighth Circuits, the Eleventh Circuit ruled that the All Writs Act may not be used as the jurisdictional predicate for removal of a state-court case that arguably undermines the effect of a previous federal judgment, settlement, or consent decree. Henson v. Ciba–Geigy Corp., 261 F.3d 1065 (11th Cir.2001). The Supreme Court has granted certiorari to resolve the conflict among the circuits. Syngenta Crop Protection, Inc. v. Henson, ___ U.S. ___, 122 S.Ct. 1062 (2002). See also MSOF Corp. v. Exxon Corp., ___ F.3d ___, 2002 WL 1339874 (5th Cir.2002) (noting the Supreme Court's granting of certiorari in Henson, and remanding case removed under All Writs Act without resolving whether such removal might be permitted in extraordinary circumstances), and Montgomery v. Aetna Plywood, Inc., 231 F.3d 399, 411, n. 4 (7th Cir.2000) (reconceptualizing All Writs Act removal as based on ancillary jurisdiction). The Seventh Circuit's view is discussed above in connection with the discussion of supplemental jurisdiction at page 154 of the main volume.

Page 250. Add to Footnote 9

The Third Circuit has held that ERISA does not completely preempt state-law malpractice claims against an HMO. In re U.S. Healthcare, 193 F.3d 151 (3d Cir.1999). In BLAB T.V. of Mobile v. Comcast Cable Communications, Inc., 182 F.3d 851 (11th Cir.1999), the Eleventh Circuit rejected a complete preemption argument based on § 612 of the Cable Communications Policy Act of 1984.

Page 274. Add to Footnote 35

In Sherrod v. American Airlines, Inc., 132 F.3d 1112 (5th Cir.1998), the Fifth Circuit held that § 1445(c) made a claim arising under Texas workers' compensation law nonremovable even when joined to a related federal-question claim, and thus within the supplemental rather than diversity jurisdiction of the district court to which it had been removed. Unaccountably the court of appeals ordered remand only of the workers' compensation claim, and affirmed a judgment on the merits of the federal-question claim to which it had been joined. The only removal statute authorizing such a partial remand is § 1441(c), which the court did not reference and which in any event was clearly inapplicable, since the workers' compensation claim and the federal-question claim were patently not "separate and independent." For a less dubious application of § 1441(c), although one in which the conclusion that the relevant claims were "separate and independent" is certainly open to challenge, see Lanford v. Prince George's County, Md., 175 F.Supp.2d 797 (D.Md.2001).

Page 278. Add to Footnote 37

See Blumenkopf, Pett & Metta, Fighting Fraudulent Joinder: Proving the Impossible and Preserving Your Corporate Client's Right to a Federal Forum, 24 Am.J. Trial Advocacy 297 (2000).

Page 284. Add to Footnote 48

Recent cases are in conflict as to whether the right to remove is waived if the defendant files a motion to dismiss in state court before filing the notice of removal. In Somoano v. Ryder Systems, Inc. 985 F.Supp. 1476 (S.D.Fla.1998), the court held that there was no waiver when the motion to dismiss was filed within the 20 days required for a responsive pleading under state law, and the notice of removal was filed within the longer 30-day period permitted by § 1446(b). But other reported cases have held that filing a motion to dismiss may indicate clear and unequivocal intent to litigate in state court. See Heafitz v. Interfirst Bank of Dallas, 711 F.Supp. 92 (S.D.N.Y.1989); Scholz v. RDV Sports, Inc., 821 F.Supp. 1469 (M.D.Fla.1993). Merely filing an answer, however, does not waive the right of removal. See, e.g., Gore v. Stenson, 616 F.Supp. 895 (S.D.Tex.1984); Miami Herald Publishing Co. v. Ferre, 606 F.Supp. 122 (S.D.Fla.1984). In Jacko v. Thorn Americas, Inc., 121 F. Supp. 2d 574 (E.D.Tex.2000), the right of removal was held to have been waived by the filing and argument of a motion for summary judgment. See also Johnson, Removal and the Special Appearance—Which to Do First?, 19 Rev.Litig. 25 (2000); Musalli, Tick, Tock: Rules on the Removal Clock, 19 Rev.Litig. 47 (2000).

Page 284. Add to Footnote 50

The "right of revival" recognized in the Wilson case was given effect in Johnson v. Heublein, Inc., 982 F.Supp. 438 (S.D.Miss. 1997).

An amended complaint dropped the only claim against a nondiverse defendant. The remaining defendant then removed the case pursuant to the second paragraph of § 1446(b). At the time of removal the nondiverse defendant remained a party to an unresolved counterclaim. In an interesting but questionable decision that was insulated from appellate review by § 1447(d), the district court held that the continuing presence in the litigation of the former defendant as a counterclaiming nondiverse party destroyed diversity for removal purposes, that dismissal or remand of only the claim by the nondiverse counterclaimant was not permissible, and that the entire case should be remanded as nonremovable. Bristol–Meyers Squibb Co. v. Safety National Casualty Corp., 43 F.Supp.2d 734 (E.D.Tex. 1999).

Page 285. Add to Footnote 51

In a case in which the plaintiff's state court complaint sought only $70,000 in damages, a split panel of the Fifth Circuit has ruled that when the plaintiff responded to the defendant's $5,000 settlement offer with a $250,000 counteroffer, the tendering of the counteroffer was an "other paper" sufficient to start the 30–day removal clock ticking and to bar removal after that 30–day period had ended. Addo v. Globe Life & Accident Ins. Co., 230 F.3d 759 (5th Cir. 2000).

Successive notices of removal are not barred by 28 U.S.C. § 1446(b). In an opinion by Judge Easterbrook, the Seventh Circuit held that § 1446(b)'s reference to possible changes in the removal status of a case that is not initially removable provides clear statutory support for permitting later removal (under changed circumstances) of a case previously found unremovable. Benson v. SI Handling Systems, Inc., 188 F.3d 780 (7th Cir.1999).

Page 288.

There is a typographical error in the text of the first sentence of 28 U.S.C. § 1447(c) as reprinted at lines 4–5. After the words "on the basis of any defect" the words "in removal procedure" should be striken. The correct language of the first sentence of § 1447(c) is as follows:

> (c) A motion to remand the case on the basis of any defect other than lack of subject matter jurisdiction must be made within 30 days after the filing of the notice of removal under section 1446(a).

Page 288. Add to Footnote 58

In an opinion by Chief Judge Posner, the Seventh Circuit has denied preclusive effect to remand orders premised on a lack of federal subject-matter jurisdiction that are nonreviewable under § 1447(d). Health Cost Controls of Illinois, Inc. v. Washington, 187 F.3d 703 (7th Cir.1999).

Disapproving a line of contrary cases from the district courts, the first circuit to rule on the issue has held that a magistrate judge whose exercise of civil jurisdiction is not based on the parties' consent under 28 U.S.C. § 636(c)(1), and whose authority is thus limited to "nondispositive pretrial orders" under § 636(b), has no authority to remand a removed case. Such an unauthorized remand order is equivalent to a dismissal and is appealable notwithstanding § 1447(d). In re U.S. Healthcare, 159 F.3d 142 (3d Cir.1998).

Page 289. Insert before Burroughs v. Palumbo

Murphy Brothers, Inc. v. Michetti Pipe Stringing, Inc.

Supreme Court of the United States, 1999.
526 U.S. 344, 119 S.Ct. 1322, 143 L.Ed.2d 448.

■ JUSTICE GINSBURG delivered the opinion of the Court.

This case concerns the time within which a defendant named in a state-court action may remove the action to a federal court. The governing provision is 28 U.S.C. § 1446(b), which specifies, in relevant part, that the removal notice "shall be filed within thirty days after the receipt by the defendant, through service or otherwise, of a copy of the [complaint]." The question presented is whether the named defendant must be officially summoned to appear in the action before the time to remove begins to run. Or, may the 30–day period start earlier, on the named defendant's receipt, before service of official process, of a "courtesy copy" of the filed complaint faxed by counsel for the plaintiff?

We read Congress' provisions for removal in light of a bedrock principle: An individual or entity named as a defendant is not obliged to engage in litigation unless notified of the action, and brought under a court's authority, by formal process. Accordingly, we hold that a named defendant's time to remove is triggered by simultaneous service of the summons and complaint, or receipt of the complaint, "through service or otherwise," after and apart from service of the summons, but not by mere receipt of the complaint unattended by any formal service.

I

On January 26, 1996, respondent Michetti Pipe Stringing, Inc. (Michetti), filed a complaint in Alabama state court seeking damages for an alleged breach of contract and fraud by petitioner Murphy Bros., Inc. (Murphy). Michetti did not serve Murphy at that time, but three days later it faxed a "courtesy copy" of the file-stamped complaint to one of Murphy's vice presidents. The parties then engaged in settlement discussions until February 12, 1996, when Michetti officially served Murphy under local law by certified mail.

On March 13, 1996 (30 days after service but 44 days after receiving the faxed copy of the complaint), Murphy removed the case under 28 U.S.C. § 1441 to the United States District Court for the Northern District of Alabama.[1] Michetti moved to remand the case to the state court on the ground that Murphy filed the removal notice 14 days too late. The notice of removal had not been filed within 30 days of the date on which Murphy's vice president received the facsimile transmission. Consequently, Michetti asserted, the removal was untimely under 28 U.S.C. § 1446(b), which provides:

> "The notice of removal of a civil action or proceeding shall be filed within thirty days after the receipt by the defendant, *through service or otherwise*, of a copy of the initial pleading setting forth the claim for relief upon which such action or proceeding is based, or within thirty days after the service of summons upon the defendant if such initial pleading has then been filed in court and is not required to be served on the defendant, whichever period is shorter." (Emphasis added.)

The District Court denied the remand motion on the ground that the 30–day removal period did not commence until Murphy was officially

---

1. Murphy invoked the jurisdiction of the Federal District Court under 28 U.S.C. § 1332 based on diversity of citizenship. Michetti is a Canadian company with its principal place of business in Alberta, Canada; Murphy is an Illinois corporation with its principal place of business in that State.

served with a summons. The court observed that the phrase "or otherwise" was added to § 1446(b) in 1949 to govern removal in States where an action is commenced merely by the service of a summons, without any requirement that the complaint be served or even filed contemporaneously. Accordingly, the District Court said, the phrase had "no field of operation" in States such as Alabama, where the complaint must be served along with the summons.

On interlocutory appeal permitted pursuant to 28 U.S.C. § 1292(b), the Court of Appeals for the Eleventh Circuit reversed and remanded, instructing the District Court to remand the action to state court. 125 F.3d 1396, 1399 (1997). The Eleventh Circuit held that "the clock starts to tick upon the defendant's receipt of a copy of the filed initial pleading." Id., at 1397. "By and large," the appellate court wrote, "our analysis begins and ends with" the words "receipt . . . or otherwise." Id., at 1397–1398 (emphasis deleted). Because lower courts have divided on the question whether service of process is a prerequisite for the running of the 30–day removal period under § 1446(b), we granted certiorari. . . .

II

Service of process, under longstanding tradition in our system of justice, is fundamental to any procedural imposition on a named defendant. At common law, the writ of capias ad respondendum directed the sheriff to secure the defendant's appearance by taking him into custody. See 1 J. Moore, Moore's Federal Practice ¶ 0.6[2.–2], p. 212 (2d ed. 1996) ("[T]he three royal courts, Exchequer, Common Pleas, and King's Bench . . . obtained an in personam jurisdiction over the defendant in the same manner through the writ of capias ad respondendum."). The requirement that a defendant be brought into litigation by official service is the contemporary counterpart to that writ. See International Shoe Co. v. Washington, 326 U.S. 310, 316 (1945) ("[T]he capias ad respondendum has given way to personal service of summons or other form of notice.").

In the absence of service of process (or waiver of service by the defendant), a court ordinarily may not exercise power over a party the complaint names as defendant. See Omni Capital Int'l, Ltd. v. Rudolf Wolff & Co., 484 U.S. 97, 104 (1987) ("Before a . . . court may exercise personal jurisdiction over a defendant, the procedural requirement of service of summons must be satisfied."); Mississippi Publishing Corp. v. Murphree, 326 U.S. 438, 444–445 (1946) ("[S]ervice of summons is the procedure by which a court . . . asserts jurisdiction over the person of the party served."). Accordingly, one becomes a party officially, and is required to take action in that capacity, only upon service of a summons or other authority-asserting measure stating the time within which the party served must appear and defend. See Fed. Rule Civ. Proc. 4(a) ("[The summons] shall . . . state the time within which the defendant must appear and defend, and notify the defendant that failure to do so will result in a judgment by default against the defendant."); Fed. Rule Civ. Proc. 12(a)(1)(A) (a defendant shall serve an answer within 20 days of being served with the summons and complaint). Unless a named defendant agrees to waive service, the summons continues to function as the sine qua non directing an individual or entity to participate in a civil action or forgo procedural or substantive rights.

III

When Congress enacted § 1446(b), the legislators did not endeavor to break away from the traditional understanding. Prior to 1948, a defendant could remove a case any time before the expiration of her time to respond to the complaint under state law. See, e.g., 28 U.S.C. § 72 (1940 ed.). Because the time limits for responding to the complaint varied from State to State, however, the period for removal correspondingly varied. To reduce the disparity, Congress in 1948 enacted the original version of § 1446(b), which provided that "[t]he petition for removal of a civil action or proceeding may be filed within twenty days after commencement of the action or service of process, whichever is later." Act of June 25, 1948, 62 Stat. 939, as amended, 28 U.S.C. § 1446(b). According to the relevant House Report, this provision was intended to "give adequate time and operate uniformly throughout the Federal jurisdiction." H.R.Rep. No. 308, 80th Cong., 1st Sess., A135 (1947).

Congress soon recognized, however, that § 1446(b), as first framed, did not "give adequate time and operate uniformly" in all States. In States such as New York, most notably, service of the summons commenced the action, and such service could precede the filing of the complaint. Under § 1446(b) as originally enacted, the period for removal in such a State could have expired before the defendant obtained access to the complaint.

To ensure that the defendant would have access to the complaint before commencement of the removal period, Congress in 1949 enacted the current version of § 1446(b): "The petition for removal of a civil action or proceeding shall be filed within twenty days [now thirty days][2] after the receipt by the defendant, through service or otherwise, of a copy of the initial pleading setting forth the claim for relief upon which such action or proceeding is based." Act of May 24, 1949, § 83(a), 63 Stat. 101. The accompanying Senate Report explained:

> "In some States suits are begun by the service of a summons or other process without the necessity of filing any pleading until later. As the section now stands, this places the defendant in the position of having to take steps to remove a suit to Federal court before he knows what the suit is about. As said section is herein proposed to be rewritten, a defendant is not required to file his petition for removal until 20 days

---

2. Congress extended the period for removal from 20 days to 30 days in 1965. See Act of September 29, 1965, 79 Stat. 887.

after he has received (or it has been made available to him) a copy of the initial pleading filed by the plaintiff setting forth the claim upon which the suit is based and the relief prayed for. It is believed that this will meet the varying conditions of practice in all the States." S.Rep. No. 303, 81st Cong., 1st Sess., 6 (1949).

See also H.R.Rep. No. 352, 81st Cong., 1st Sess., 14 (1949) ("The first paragraph of the amendment to subsection (b) corrects [the New York problem] by providing that the petition for removal need not be filed until 20 days after the defendant has received a copy of the plaintiff's initial pleading.").[3] Nothing in the legislative history of the 1949 amendment so much as hints that Congress, in making changes to accommodate atypical state commencement and complaint filing procedures, intended to dispense with the historic function of service of process as the official trigger for responsive action by an individual or entity named defendant.[4]

IV

The Eleventh Circuit relied on the "plain meaning" of § 1446(b) that the panel perceived. See 125 F.3d, at 1398. In the Eleventh Circuit's view, because the term " '[r]eceipt' is the nominal form of 'receive,' which means broadly 'to come into possession of' or to 'acquire,' 'the phrase' '[receipt] through service or otherwise' opens a universe of means besides service for putting the defendant in possession of the complaint." Ibid. What are the dimensions of that "universe"? The Eleventh Circuit's opinion is uninformative. Nor can one tenably maintain that the words "or otherwise" provide a clue. Cf. Potter v. McCauley, 186 F.Supp. 146, 149 (D.Md.1960) ("It is not possible to state definitely in general terms the precise scope and effect of the word 'otherwise' in its context here because its proper application in particular situations will vary with state procedural requirements."); Apache Nitrogen Products, Inc. v. Harbor Ins. Co., 145 F.R.D.

3. The second half of the revised § 1446(b), providing that the petition for removal shall be filed "within twenty days after the service of summons upon the defendant if such initial pleading has then been filed in court and is not required to be served on the defendant, whichever period is shorter," § 83(b), 63 Stat. 101, was added to address the situation in States such as Kentucky, which required the complaint to be filed at the time the summons issued, but did not require service of the complaint along with the summons. See H.R.Rep. No. 352, 81st Cong., 1st Sess., 14 (1949) ("Th[e first clause of revised § 1446(b)], however, without more, would create further difficulty in those States, such as Kentucky, where suit is commenced by the filing of the plaintiff's initial pleading and the issu-

ance and service of a summons without any requirement that a copy of the pleading be served upon or otherwise furnished to the defendant. Accordingly ... the amendment provides that in such cases the petition for removal shall be filed within 20 days after the service of the summons.").

4. It is evident, too, that Congress could not have foreseen the situation posed by this case, for, as the District Court recognized, "[i]n 1949 Congress did not anticipate use of facsmile [sic] transmissions." Indeed, even the photocopy machine was not yet on the scene at that time. See 9 New Encyclopedia Britannica 400 (15th ed.1985) (noting that photocopiers "did not become available for commercial use until 1950").

674, 679 (D.Ariz.1993) ("[I]f in fact the words 'service or otherwise' had a plain meaning, the cases would not be so hopelessly split over their proper interpretation.").

The interpretation of § 1446(b) adopted here adheres to tradition, makes sense of the phrase "or otherwise," and assures defendants adequate time to decide whether to remove an action to federal court. As the court in *Potter* observed, the various state provisions for service of the summons and the filing or service of the complaint fit into one or another of four main categories. See *Potter*, 186 F.Supp., at 149. In each of the four categories, the defendant's period for removal will be no less than 30 days from service, and in some categories, it will be more than 30 days from service, depending on when the complaint is received.

As summarized in *Potter*, the possibilities are as follows. First, if the summons and complaint are served together, the 30–day period for removal runs at once. Second, if the defendant is served with the summons but the complaint is furnished to the defendant sometime after, the period for removal runs from the defendant's receipt of the complaint. Third, if the defendant is served with the summons and the complaint is filed in court, but under local rules, service of the complaint is not required, the removal period runs from the date the complaint is made available through filing. Finally, if the complaint is filed in court prior to any service, the removal period runs from the service of the summons. See ibid.

Notably, Federal Rule of Civil Procedure 81(c), amended in 1949, uses the identical "receipt through service or otherwise" language in specifying the time the defendant has to answer the complaint once the case has been removed:

> "In a removed action in which the defendant has not answered, the defendant shall answer or present the other defenses or objections available under these rules within 20 days after the receipt through service or otherwise of a copy of the initial pleading setting forth the claim for relief upon which the action or proceeding is based."

Rule 81(c) sensibly has been interpreted to afford the defendant at least 20 days after service of process to respond. See Silva v. Madison, 69 F.3d 1368, 1376–1377 (C.A.7 1995). In *Silva*, the Seventh Circuit Court of Appeals observed that "nothing . . . would justify our concluding that the drafters, in their quest for evenhandedness and promptness in the removal process, intended to abrogate the necessity for something as fundamental as service of process." Id., at 1376. In reaching this conclusion, the court distinguished an earlier decision, Roe v. O'Donohue, 38 F.3d 298 (C.A.7 1994), which held that a defendant need not receive service of process before his time for removal under § 1446(b) begins to run. See 69 F.3d, at 1376. But, as the United States maintains in its amicus curiae brief, the *Silva* court "did not adequately explain why one who has not yet lawfully been made a party to an action should be required to decide in which court system the case should be heard." If, as the Seventh Circuit rightly determined, the

27

"service or otherwise" language was not intended to abrogate the service requirement for purposes of Rule 81(c), that same language also was not intended to bypass service as a starter for § 1446(b)'s clock. The fact that the Seventh Circuit could read the phrase "or otherwise" differently in *Silva* and *Roe*, moreover, undercuts the Eleventh Circuit's position that the phrase has an inevitably "plain meaning."[5]

Furthermore, the so-called "receipt rule"—starting the time to remove on receipt of a copy of the complaint, however informally, despite the absence of any formal service—could, as the District Court recognized, operate with notable unfairness to individuals and entities in foreign nations. Because facsimile machines transmit instantaneously, but formal service abroad may take much longer than 30 days, plaintiffs "would be able to dodge the requirements of international treaties and trap foreign opponents into keeping their suits in state courts."

* * *

In sum, it would take a clearer statement than Congress has made to read its endeavor to extend removal time (by adding receipt of the complaint) to effect so strange a change—to set removal apart from all other responsive acts, to render removal the sole instance in which one's procedural rights slip away before service of a summons, i.e., before one is subject to any court's authority. Accordingly, for the reasons stated in this opinion, the judgment of the United States Court of Appeals for the Eleventh Circuit is reversed, and the case is remanded for further proceedings consistent with this opinion.

It is so ordered.

■ CHIEF JUSTICE REHNQUIST, with whom JUSTICE SCALIA and JUSTICE THOMAS join, dissenting.

Respondent faxed petitioner a copy of the file-stamped complaint in its commenced state-court action, and I believe that the receipt of this facsimile triggered the 30–day removal period under the plain language of 28 U.S.C. § 1446(b). The Court does little to explain why the plain language of the statute should not control, opting instead to superimpose a judicially

---

5. Contrary to a suggestion made at oral argument, 28 U.S.C. § 1448 does not support the Eleventh Circuit's position. That section provides that "[i]n all cases removed from any State court to any district court of the United States in which any one or more of the defendants has not been served with process or in which the service has not been perfected prior to removal . . . such process or service may be completed or new process issued in the same manner as in cases originally filed in such district court." Nothing in § 1448 requires the de-fendant to take any action. The statute simply allows the plaintiff to serve an unserved defendant or to perfect flawed service once the action has been removed. In fact, the second paragraph of § 1448, which provides that "[t]his section shall not deprive any defendant upon whom process is served after removal of his right to move to remand the case," explicitly reserves the unserved defendant's right to take action (move to remand) *after* service is perfected.

created service of process requirement onto § 1446(b). In so doing, it departs from this Court's practice of strictly construing removal and similar jurisdictional statutes. See Shamrock Oil & Gas Corp. v. Sheets, 313 U.S. 100, 108–109 (1941). Because I believe the Eleventh Circuit's analysis of the issue presented in this case was cogent and correct, see 125 F.3d 1396, 1397–1398 (1997), I would affirm the dismissal of petitioner's removal petition for the reasons stated by that court.

————

Page 292. Add to Footnote 60

It was held in Lawrence v. Chancery Court of Tennessee, 188 F.3d 687 (6th Cir.1999), that after the removal of a case the state court retains the power to assess costs incurred prior to the removal of the litigation.

CHAPTER VI

VENUE

Page 303. Add to Footnote 3

Under the rule of Camp v. Gress, 250 U.S. 308 (1919), venue is a personal privilege. When venue is laid on the basis of the residence of the defendants in a district in which all defendants do not in fact reside, only the nonresident defendant may move to dismiss under § 1391(a)(2) or § 1391(b)(2) for lack of proper venue. See generally 5A Wright & Miller, Federal Practice & Procedure: Civil 2d § 1352 (1990); 15 Wright, Miller & Cooper, Federal Practice & Procedure: Jurisdiction 2d §§ 3807, 3829 (1986).

In FS Photo, Inc. v. PictureVision, Inc., 48 F.Supp.2d 442 (D.Del.1999), the court discussed the limited scope of "fallback" venue under § 1391(b)(3), and held that it may be invoked only when there is no other district in which both venue and personal jurisdiction are proper as to all defendants.

Page 304. Add to Footnote 6

A standing question posed by any special venue provision is whether it is restrictive (specifying venue exclusive of the general venue statute, 28 U.S.C. § 1391) or permissive (supplementing the venue options provided by the general venue statute). In Cortez Byrd Chips, Inc. v. Bill Harbert Construction Co., 529 U.S. 193 (2000), the Court determined that the special venue provisions of the Federal Arbitration Act, 9 U.S.C. §§ 9–11, were permissive rather than restrictive. Thus the venue of an action to vacate or modify an arbitration award was held to have properly been laid in the district in which the relevant contract was to have been performed—a district in which venue was proper under 28 U.S.C. § 1391(a)(2)—even though it was not a district specified by 9 U.S.C. §§ 10–11, which specify that an action to vacate (§ 10) or modify (§ 11) an arbitration award may be brought in the district in which the award was made.

When different venue statutes apply to multiple claims joined in a single complaint, difficult questions of "pendent venue" may arise. See Corn, Comment, Pendent Venue: A Doctrine in Search of a Theory, 68 U.Chi.L.Rev. 931 (2001).

Page 323. Add to Footnote 12

In Posner v. Essex Insurance Co., Ltd., 178 F.3d 1209 (11th Cir.1999), the court ostensibly invoked the novel doctrine of "international abstention," but the authority to dismiss the suit in question would appear far more conventionally rooted in the power to dismiss on forum non conveniens grounds, as established in the Piper Aircraft case.

There is a "first-to-file" rule that generally leads the second court in which related litigation is pending to defer to the first court. This rule may be expressed as a venue rule, but appears to function as a form of abstention. See Cadle Co. v. Whataburger of Alice, Inc., 174 F.3d 599 (5th Cir.1999).

CHAPTER VII

JURISDICTION TO DETERMINE JURISDICTION

Page 335. Add to Footnote 4

Under 18 U.S.C. § 3742(a)(1), a defendant may appeal the sentence received for a crime if the sentence "was imposed in violation of law." The Ninth Circuit held that the sentence in question was illegal. Reversing the Ninth Circuit on this point, the Supreme Court paused to explain why this did not abrogate its appellate jurisdiction."Although we ultimately conclude that respondent's sentence was not 'imposed in violation of law' and therefore that § 3742(a)(1) does not authorize an appeal in a case of this kind, it is familiar law that a federal court always has jurisdiction to determine its own jurisdiction. United States v. United Mine Workers, 330 U.S. 258, 291 (1947)." United States v. Ruiz, 536 U.S. ___, ___ 122 S.Ct. 2450, 2451 (2002).

Page 343.

The official report of the Ruhrgas case appears at 526 U.S. 574.

Page 349. Add to Footnote 14

The circuits are divided as to whether a case may be dismissed with prejudice as a procedural sanction if the district court lacks subject-matter jurisdiction of the case. Two circuits have said no. Hernandez v. Conriv Realty Associates, 182 F.3d 121 (2d Cir. 1999); In re Orthopedic "Bone Screw" Products Liability Litigation, 132 F.3d 152 (3d Cir.1997). The Ninth Circuit has ruled otherwise, deeming a dismissal ordered as a procedural sanction to be collateral to the merits. In re Exxon Valdez, 102 F.3d 429 (9th Cir.1996).

In Calderon v. Ashmus, 523 U.S. 740, 745 n. 2 (1998), the Court held that a challenge to the judicial power of a federal court under Article III must be resolved before considering whether the court lacks jurisdiction under the Eleventh Amendment. Heeding this declaration, the Court issued an order in Vermont Agency of Natural Resources v. United States, 528 U.S. 1015 (1999), a case in which certiorari had been granted to determine the Eleventh Amendment status of a suit against a state filed by a private party under the False Claims Act, directing the parties "to file supplemental briefs addressing the following question: 'Does a private person have standing under Article III to litigate claims of fraud upon the government?' " The Court eventually decided that individuals have Article III standing to bring False Claim Act suits as partial assignees of the federal government's claims for damages, but avoided deciding the Eleventh Amendment issue by holding that the statute does not authorize such a suit to be brought in federal court by a private party against a state. Vermont Agency of Natural Resources v. United States, 529 U.S. 765 (2000), also discussed above in connection with p. 49, n. 28, and below in connection with p. 418, n. 36.

See Steinman, After *Steel Co.*: Hypothetical Jurisdiction in the Federal Appellate Courts, 58 Wash. & Lee L.Rev. 855 (2001).

CHAPTER VIII

CONFLICTS BETWEEN STATE AND NATIONAL JUDICIAL SYSTEMS

SECTION 1. STATE ENFORCEMENT OF FEDERAL LAW

Page 363. Add to Footnote 7

A trio of new cases on the constitutional scope of state sovereign immunity were decided at the end of the October 1998 Term. These cases—Florida Prepaid Postsecondary Education Board v. College Savings Bank (College Savings Bank I), 527 U.S. 627 (1999), College Savings Bank v. Florida Prepaid Postsecondary Education Board (College Savings Bank II), 527 U.S. 666 (1999), and Alden v. Maine, 527 U.S. 706 (1999)—are also discussed below in connection with p. 418, n. 36. They invite attention to the precise terms of the question presented to the Court in Howlett (at p. 355 of the main volume), and of the Court's answer to that question (at p. 366) (emphasis added):

> ... The question in this case is whether a state law defense of "sovereign immunity" is available to *a school board otherwise subject to suit in a Florida court* even though *such a defense would not be available if the action had been brought in a federal forum.*

> . . .

> ... We conclude that whether the question is framed in pre-emption terms, as petitioner would have it, or in the obligation to assume jurisdiction over a "federal" cause of action, as respondents would have it, the Florida court's refusal to entertain one discrete category of § 1983 claims, *when the court entertains similar state law actions against state*

defendants, violates the Supremacy Clause.

Howlett thus dealt with the federal liabilities of local governmental officials and entities that were concededly enforceable in federal court, but which state courts were refusing to enforce under principles of state sovereign immunity that did not bar suit against such defendants on similar state-law grounds. Howlett did not address the power of Congress to impose a federal liability directly on nonconsenting states (as opposed to local governmental entities) that could not be enforced against such states in federal court by dint of the Eleventh Amendment and related principles of state sovereign immunity implicitly protected by Article III's underlying limitation of federal judicial power. The three new decisions bear directly on these issues, and suggest that the force of the Howlett decision may not extend far beyond its particular facts.

Alden held that the Tenth Amendment prohibits Congress from imposing federal liabilities enforceable by private suit against nonconsenting states in their own courts. Although the enforcement power conferred on Congress by § 5 of the later-enacted Fourteenth Amendment trumps the Eleventh Amendment (and presumably the Tenth as well) to allow Congress to authorize private suit to enforce such liabilities in the federal courts (and, thus under Howlett, presumably in state courts as well), the College Savings Bank cases took a quite narrow view of the scope of congressional power to enforce the Fourteenth Amendment. That narrow view has since been refined and applied in Kimel v. Florida Board of Regents, 528 U.S. 62 (2000), and Board of Trustees of the University of Alabama v. Garrett, 531 U.S. 356 (2001), discussed below in connection with p. 418, n. 36, and United States v. Morrison, 529 U.S. 598 (2000), discussed above in connection with p. 242, n. 2.

How broad is the power of Congress, incident to its regulation of commerce, to regulate the procedural rules applied by state courts in civil litigation that might affect commerce? And is such power as Congress may possess limited to state-court adjudication of claims for relief grounded in federal law, or does it extend even to state-court litigation of claims arising solely under state law? See Bellia, Federal Regulation of State Court Procedures, 110 Yale L.J. 947 (2001).

Section 4.   Federal Actions to Restrain State Officers

Page 398. Add to Footnote 23

In Brown & Root, Inc. v. Breckenridge, 211 F.3d 194 (4th Cir.2000), the Rooker–Feldman doctrine was held to bar a federal court from considering a suit to compel arbitration under the Federal Arbitration Act, 9 U.S.C. § 4, when the state courts had previously denied a motion to arbitrate the same dispute.

In a case that allowed an abortion clinic to proceed with its challenge to test the constitutionality of state antiabortion laws, the Eleventh Circuit held that a showing of imminent enforcement of an allegedly unconstitutional state law is not required in a suit seeking prospective injunctive relief against a state officer under the doctrine of Ex parte Young. Summit Medical Associates, P.C. v. Pryor, 180 F.3d 1326 (11th Cir.1999).

Page 418. Add to Footnote 36

The bloc of five Justices who formed the majority in Seminole Tribe has extended the reasoning of that case to hold that Congress lacks Article I power to required nonconsenting states to adjudicate in their own courts private federal suits to enforce concededly constitutional obligations imposed on states by federal law, notwithstanding that such obligations could be enforced—if far less efficiently—by suits in federal courts brought by the United States itself on behalf of the wronged individuals. See Alden v. Maine, 527 U.S. 706 (1999), which along with Florida Prepaid Postsecondary Education Board v. College Savings Bank (College Savings Bank I), 527 U.S. 627, and College Savings Bank v. Florida Prepaid Postsecondary Education Board (College Savings Bank II), 527 U.S. 666 is also discussed above in connection with p. 363, n. 7.

Alden is uncompromising in its reaffirmation and extension of the reasoning of Seminole Tribe. It held that Congress lacked the power to compel state courts to entertain suits against a state by state employees, who had been denied the overtime pay to which they were entitled under the federal Fair Labor Standards Act (FLSA).

We have … sometimes referred to the States' immunity from suit as "Eleventh Amendment immunity." The phrase is convenient shorthand but something of a misnomer, for the sovereign immunity of the States neither derives from nor is limited by the terms of the Eleventh Amendment. Rather, as the Constitution's structure, and its history, and the authoritative interpretations by this Court make clear, the States' immunity from suit is a fundamental aspect of the sovereignty which the States enjoyed before the ratification of the Constitution, and which they retain today (either literally or by virtue of their admission into the Union upon an equal footing with

35 usc

33

the other States) except as altered by the plan of the Convention or certain constitutional Amendments.

. . . Any doubt regarding the constitutional role of the States as sovereign entities is removed by the Tenth Amendment, which, like the other provisions of the Bill of Rights, was enacted to allay lingering concerns about the extent of the national power.

. . .

. . . The State of Maine has not questioned Congress' power to prescribe substantive rules of federal law to which it must comply. Despite an initial good-faith disagreement about the requirements of the FLSA, it is conceded by all that the State has altered its conduct so that its compliance with federal law cannot now be questioned. The Solicitor General of the United States has appeared before this Court, however, and asserted that the federal interest in compensating the State's employees for alleged past violations of federal law is so compelling that sovereign State of Maine must be stripped of its immunity and subjected to suit in its own courts by its own employees. Yet, despite specific statutory authorization, 29 U.S.C. § 216(c), the United States apparently found the same interests insufficient to justify sending even a single attorney to Maine to prosecute this litigation. The difference between a suit by the United States on behalf of the employees and a suit by the employees implicates a rule that the National Government must itself deem the case of sufficient importance to take action against a State; and history, precedent, and the structure of the Constitution make clear that, under the plan of the Convention, the States have consented to suits of the first kind but not of the second.

527 U.S. at 713–714, 759–760.

By the same 5–4 majority, the Court held the same day in the two College Savings Bank cases that neither the express liability imposed on states by the Patent and Plant Variety Protection Remedy Clarification Act, nor that imposed by the Trademark Remedy Clarification Act (amending the Lanham Act), could be sustained despite

the reliance of Congress on legislative power conferred by § 5 of the Fourteenth Amendment as well as the patent and commerce clauses of Article I.

In College Savings Bank I the Court held that Congress had failed to show that stripping states of their sovereign immunity from patent-infringement suits was necessary to remedy the Fourteenth Amendment violation of depriving patentees of property without "due process of law," since "Congress itself said nothing about the existence or adequacy of state remedies. . . ." 527 U.S. at 644.

The historical record and the scope of coverage therefore make it clear that the Patent Remedy Act cannot be sustained under § 5 of the Fourteenth Amendment. The examples of States avoiding liability for patent infringement by pleading sovereign immunity in a federal-court patent action are scarce enough, but any plausible argument that such action on the part of the State deprived patentees of property and left them without a remedy under state law is scarcer still. The statute's apparent and more basic aims were to provide a uniform remedy and to place States on the same footing as private parties under that regime. These are proper Article I concerns, but that Article does not give Congress the power to enact such legislation after *Seminole Tribe.*

527 U.S. at 647–648.

In College Savings Bank II, the Court reached a similar conclusion as to the Fourteenth Amendment argument, but on different grounds. The Court held that a trademark, unlike a patent, confers no property right that the Due Process Clause protects. 527 U.S. at 672–673. The Court then held similarly unavailing the argument that by engaging in commercial activity that infringed the trademark of competitor, Florida had " 'impliedly' or 'constructively' waived its immunity from Lanham Act suit." 527 U.S. at 676. Calling the Parden case "an elliptical opinion that stands at the nadir of our waiver (and, for that matter, sovereign immunity) jurisprudence," id., the Court declared that "the constructive-waiver experiment of *Parden* was ill conceived, and we see no merit in attempting to salvage any remnant of it." 527 U.S. at 680.

Given how anomalous it is to speak of the "constructive waiver" of a constitutionally protected privilege, it is not surprising that the very cornerstone of the *Parden* opinion was the notion that state sovereign immunity is not constitutionally grounded.... Our more recent decision in *Seminole Tribe* expressly repudiates that proposition, and in formally overruling *Parden* we do no more than make explicit what that case implied.

527 U.S. at 682–683.

See Symposium: State Sovereign Immunity and the Eleventh Amendment, 75 Notre Dame L.Rev. 817 (2000), Vázquez, Sovereign Immunity, Due Process, and the *Alden* Trilogy, 109 Yale L.J. 1927 (2000); Symposium, Shifting the Balance of Power? The Supreme Court, Federalism, and State Sovereign Immunity, 53 Stan. L.Rev. 1115 (2001); Fitzgerald, Comment, State Sovereign Immunity: Searching for Stability, 48 UCLA L.Rev. 1203 (2001); Zietlow, Federalism's Paradox: The Spending Power and Waiver of Sovereign Immunity, 37 Wake Forest L.Rev. 141 (2002).

Congress lacks the power under the Fourteenth Amendment to abrogate state sovereign immunity with respect to suits under the Age Discrimination in Employment Act (ADEA), Kimel v. Florida Board of Regents, 528 U.S. 62 (2000), or the Americans with Disabilities Act (ADA), Board of Trustees of the University of Alabama v. Garrett, 531 U.S. 356 (2001).

In Vermont Agency of Natural Resources v. United States, 529 U.S. 765 (2000), discussed below in connection with p. 49, n. 28, and p. 349, n. 14, the Court expressed "serious doubt" whether a private party could be authorized to bring a qui tam suit against a state under the False Claims Act, but held that the statute did not purport to grant such authority and thus left the Eleventh Amendment issue formally unresolved.

Congress can and has demanded constructive waiver of state sovereign immunity under Art. I's spending clause as a condition of state receipt of Title IX funds. Litman v. George Mason University, 186 F.3d 544 (4th Cir.1999). A state university's participation in a federal student loan program has likewise been held to waive the state's immunity from discharge of the loan in federal bankruptcy proceedings. Innes v. Kansas State University, 184 F.3d 1275 (10th Cir.1999). The Ninth Circuit has held that a state agency waived its Eleventh Amendment immunity by actively participating in extensive pretrial activities, rendering untimely and ineffective the immunity asserted for the first time on the opening day of trial. Hill v. Blind Industries and Services of Maryland, 179 F.3d 754 (9th Cir.1999).

Page 418. Insert after Seminole Tribe of Florida v. Florida

Federal Maritime Commission v. South Carolina State Ports Authority

Supreme Court of the United States, 2002.
535 U.S. ___, 122 S.Ct. 1864, ___ L.Ed.2d ___.

■ JUSTICE THOMAS delivered the opinion of the Court.

This case presents the question whether state sovereign immunity precludes petitioner Federal Maritime Commission (FMC or Commission) from adjudicating a private party's complaint that a state-run port has violated the Shipping Act of 1984, 46 U.S.C.App. § 1701 et seq. (1994 ed. and Supp. V). We hold that state sovereign immunity bars such an adjudicative proceeding.

I

On five occasions, South Carolina Maritime Services, Inc. (Maritime Services), asked respondent South Carolina State Ports Authority (SCSPA) for permission to berth a cruise ship, the M/V *Tropic Sea,* at the SCSPA's port facilities in Charleston, South Carolina. Maritime Services intended to offer cruises on the M/V *Tropic Sea* originating from the Port of Charleston. Some of these cruises would stop in the Bahamas while others would merely travel in international waters before returning to Charleston with no intervening ports of call. On all of these trips, passengers would be permitted to participate in gambling activities while on board.

The SCSPA repeatedly denied Maritime Services' requests, contending that it had an established policy of denying berths in the Port of Charleston to vessels whose primary purpose was gambling. As a result, Maritime Services filed a complaint with the FMC, contending that the SCSPA's refusal to provide berthing space to the M/V *Tropic Sea* violated the Shipping Act. Maritime Services alleged in its complaint that the SCSPA had implemented its antigambling policy in a discriminatory fashion by providing berthing space in Charleston to two Carnival Cruise Lines vessels even though Carnival offered gambling activities on these ships. Maritime Services therefore complained that the SCSPA had unduly and unreasonably preferred Carnival over Maritime Services in violation of 46 U.S.C.App. § 1709(d)(4) (1994 ed., Supp. V), and unreasonably refused to deal or negotiate with Maritime Services in violation of § 1709(b)(10). App. 14–15. It further alleged that the SCSPA's unlawful actions had inflicted upon Maritime Services a "loss of profits, loss of earnings, loss of sales, and loss of business opportunities." Id., at 15.

To remedy its injuries, Maritime Services prayed that the FMC: (1) seek a temporary restraining order and preliminary injunction in the United States District Court for the District of South Carolina "enjoining [the SCSPA] from utilizing its discriminatory practice to refuse to provide berthing space and passenger services to Maritime Services;"[7] (2) direct the SCSPA to pay reparations to Maritime Services as well as interest and reasonable attorneys' fees;[8] (3) issue an order commanding, among other

7. See § 1710(h)(1) (1994 ed.) ("In connection with any investigation conducted under this section, the Commission may bring suit in a district court of the United States to enjoin conduct in violation of this chapter. Upon a showing that standards for granting injunctive relief by courts of equity are met and after notice to the defendant, the court may grant a temporary restraining order or preliminary injunction for a period not to exceed 10 days after the Commission has issued an order disposing of the issues under investigation. Any such suit shall be brought in a district in which the defendant resides or transacts business").

8. See § 1710(g) (1994 ed., Supp. V) ("For any complaint filed within 3 years after the cause of action accrued, the Commission shall, upon petition of the complainant and after notice and hearing, direct payment of reparations to the complainant for actual injury (which, for purposes of this subsection, also includes the loss of interest at commercial rates compounded from the date of injury) caused by a violation of this chapter plus reasonable attorney's fees").

things, the SCSPA to cease and desist from violating the Shipping Act; and (4) award Maritime Services "such other and further relief as is just and proper." Id., at 16.

Consistent with the FMC's Rules of Practice and Procedure, Maritime Services' complaint was referred to an administrative law judge (ALJ). . . . The SCSPA then filed an answer, maintaining, inter alia, that it had adhered to its antigambling policy in a nondiscriminatory manner. It also filed a motion to dismiss, asserting, as relevant, that the SCSPA, as an arm of the State of South Carolina, was "entitled to Eleventh Amendment immunity" from Maritime Services' suit. App. 41. The SCSPA argued that "the Constitution prohibits Congress from passing a statute authorizing Maritime Services to file [this] Complaint before the Commission and, thereby, sue the State of South Carolina for damages and injunctive relief." Id., at 44.

The ALJ agreed, concluding that recent decisions of this Court "interpreting the 11th Amendment and State sovereign immunity from *private* suits ... require [d] that [Maritime Services'] complaint be dismissed." App. to Pet. for Cert. 49a (emphasis in original). Relying on Seminole Tribe of Fla. v. Florida, 517 U.S. 44 (1996), in which we held that Congress, pursuant to its Article I powers, cannot abrogate state sovereign immunity, the ALJ reasoned that "[i]f federal courts that are established under Article III of the Constitution must respect States' 11th Amendment immunity and Congress is powerless to override the States' immunity under Article I of the Constitution, it is irrational to argue that an agency like the Commission, created under an Article I statute, is free to disregard the 11th Amendment or its related doctrine of State immunity from *private* suits." App. to Pet. for Cert. 59a (emphasis in original). The ALJ noted, however, that his decision did not deprive the FMC of its "authority to look into [Maritime Services'] allegations of Shipping Act violations and enforce the Shipping Act." Id., at 60a. For example, the FMC could institute its own formal investigatory proceeding, see 46 CFR § 502.282 (2001), or refer Maritime Services' allegations to its Bureau of Enforcement, App. to Pet. for Cert. 60a–61a.

While Maritime Services did not appeal the ALJ's dismissal of its complaint, the FMC on its own motion decided to review the ALJ's ruling to consider whether state sovereign immunity from private suits extends to proceedings before the Commission. It concluded that "[t]he doctrine of state sovereign immunity ... is meant to cover proceedings before judicial tribunals, whether Federal or state, not executive branch administrative agencies like the Commission." Id., at 33a. As a result, the FMC held that sovereign immunity did not bar the Commission from adjudicating private complaints against state-run ports and reversed the ALJ's decision dismissing Maritime Services' complaint. Id., at 35a.

The SCSPA filed a petition for review, and the United States Court of Appeals for the Fourth Circuit reversed. Observing that "any proceeding where a federal officer adjudicates disputes between private parties and unconsenting states would not have passed muster at the time of the Constitution's passage nor after the ratification of the Eleventh Amendment," the Court of Appeals reasoned that "[s]uch an adjudication is equally as invalid today, whether the forum be a state court, a federal court, or a federal administrative agency." 243 F.3d 165, 173 (C.A.4 2001). Reviewing the "precise nature" of the procedures employed by the FMC for resolving private complaints, the Court of Appeals concluded that the proceeding "walks, talks, and squawks very much like a lawsuit" and that "[i]ts placement within the Executive Branch cannot blind us to the fact that the proceeding is truly an adjudication." Id., at 174. The Court of Appeals therefore held that because the SCSPA is an arm of the State of South Carolina, sovereign immunity precluded the FMC from adjudicating Maritime Services' complaint, and remanded the case with instructions that it be dismissed. Id., at 179.

We granted the FMC's petition for certiorari, 534 U.S. 971 (2001), and now affirm.

II

Dual sovereignty is a defining feature of our Nation's constitutional blueprint. See Gregory v. Ashcroft, 501 U.S. 452, 457 (1991). States, upon ratification of the Constitution, did not consent to become mere appendages of the Federal Government. Rather, they entered the Union "with their sovereignty intact." Blatchford v. Native Village of Noatak, 501 U.S. 775, 779 (1991). An integral component of that "residuary and inviolable sovereignty," The Federalist No. 39, p. 245 (C. Rossiter ed. 1961) (J. Madison), retained by the States is their immunity from private suits. Reflecting the widespread understanding at the time the Constitution was drafted, Alexander Hamilton explained,

> "It is inherent in the nature of sovereignty not to be amenable to the suit of an individual *without its consent*. This is the general sense and the general practice of mankind; and the exemption, as one of the attributes of sovereignty, is now enjoyed by the government of every State of the Union. Unless, therefore, there is a surrender of this immunity in the plan of the convention, it will remain with the States...." Id., No. 81, at 487–488 (emphasis in original).

States, in ratifying the Constitution, did surrender a portion of their inherent immunity by consenting to suits brought by sister States or by the Federal Government. See Alden v. Maine, 527 U.S. 706, 755 (1999). Nevertheless, the Convention did not disturb States' immunity from private suits, thus firmly enshrining this principle in our constitutional framework. "The leading advocates of the Constitution assured the people in no uncertain terms that the Constitution would not strip the States of sovereign immunity." Id., at 716.

The States' sovereign immunity, however, fell into peril in the early days of our Nation's history when this Court held in Chisholm v. Georgia, 2 Dall. [2 U.S.] 419 (1793), that Article III authorized citizens of one State to sue another State in federal court. The "decision 'fell upon the country with a profound shock.'" *Alden*, supra, at 720, quoting 1 C. Warren, The Supreme Court in United States History 96 (rev. ed.1926). In order to overturn *Chisholm,* Congress quickly passed the Eleventh Amendment and the States ratified it speedily. The Amendment clarified that "[t]he judicial Power of the United States shall not be construed to extend to any suit in law or equity, commenced or prosecuted against one of the United States by Citizens of another State, or by Citizens or Subjects of any Foreign State." We have since acknowledged that the *Chisholm* decision was erroneous. See, e.g., *Alden*, 527 U.S., at 721–722.

Instead of explicitly memorializing the full breadth of the sovereign immunity retained by the States when the Constitution was ratified, Congress chose in the text of the Eleventh Amendment only to "address the specific provisions of the Constitution that had raised concerns during the ratification debates and formed the basis of the *Chisholm* decision." Id., at 723. As a result, the Eleventh Amendment does not define the scope of the States' sovereign immunity; it is but one particular exemplification of that immunity. Cf. *Blatchford*, supra, at 779 ("[W]e have understood the Eleventh Amendment to stand not so much for what it says, but for the presupposition of our constitutional structure which it confirms").

III

We now consider whether the sovereign immunity enjoyed by States as part of our constitutional framework applies to adjudications conducted by the FMC. Petitioner FMC and respondent United States[9] initially maintain that the Court of Appeals erred because sovereign immunity only shields States from exercises of "judicial power" and FMC adjudications are not judicial proceedings. As support for their position, they point to the text of the Eleventh Amendment and contend that "[t]he Amendment's reference to 'judicial Power' and 'to any suit in law or equity' clearly mark it as an immunity from judicial process." Brief for United States 15.

For purposes of this case, we will assume, arguendo, that in adjudicating complaints filed by private parties under the Shipping Act, the FMC does not exercise the judicial power of the United States. Such an assump-

---

9. While the United States is a party to this case and agrees with the FMC that state sovereign immunity does not preclude the Commission from adjudicating Maritime Services' complaint against the SCSPA, it is nonetheless a respondent because it did not seek review of the Court of Appeals' decision below. See this Court's Rule 12.6. The United States instead opposed the FMC's petition for certiorari. See Brief for United States in Opposition.

tion, however, does not end our inquiry as this Court has repeatedly held that the sovereign immunity enjoyed by the States extends beyond the literal text of the Eleventh Amendment.[10] See, e.g., *Alden*, supra (holding that sovereign immunity shields States from private suits in state courts pursuant to federal causes of action); *Blatchford*, supra (applying state sovereign immunity to suits by Indian tribes); Principality of Monaco v. Mississippi, 292 U.S. 313 (1934) (applying state sovereign immunity to suits by foreign nations); Ex parte New York, 256 U.S. 490 (1921) (applying state sovereign immunity to admiralty proceedings); Smith v. Reeves, 178 U.S. 436 (1900) (applying state sovereign immunity to suits by federal corporations); Hans v. Louisiana, 134 U.S. 1 (1890) (applying state sovereign immunity to suits by a State's own citizens under federal-question jurisdiction). Adhering to that well-reasoned precedent, see Part II, supra, we must determine whether the sovereign immunity embedded in our constitutional structure and retained by the States when they joined the Union extends to FMC adjudicative proceedings.

A

"[L]ook[ing] first to evidence of the original understanding of the Constitution," *Alden*, 527 U.S., at 741, as well as early congressional practice, see id., at 743–744, we find a relatively barren historical record, from which the parties draw radically different conclusions. Petitioner FMC, for instance, argues that state sovereign immunity should not extend to administrative adjudications because "[t]here is no evidence that state immunity from the adjudication of complaints by *executive officers* was an established principle at the time of the adoption of the Constitution." Brief for Petitioner 28 (emphasis in original). The SCSPA, on the other hand, asserts that it is more relevant that "Congress did not attempt to subject the States to private suits before federal administrative tribunals" during the early days of our Republic. Brief for Respondent SCSPA 19.

In truth, the relevant history does not provide direct guidance for our inquiry. The Framers, who envisioned a limited Federal Government, could not have anticipated the vast growth of the administrative state. See *Alden*, supra, at 807 (SOUTER, J., dissenting) ("The proliferation of Government, State and Federal, would amaze the Framers, and the administrative state with its reams of regulations would leave them rubbing their eyes"). Because formalized administrative adjudications were all but unheard of in the late 18th century and early 19th century, the dearth of specific evidence

---

10. To the extent that JUSTICE BREYER, looking to the text of the Eleventh Amendment, suggests that sovereign immunity only shields States from the " 'the judicial power of the United States,' " post, at [54] (dissenting opinion), he "engage[s] in the type of a historical literalism we have rejected in interpreting the scope of the States' sovereign immunity since the discredited decision in *Chisholm*," Alden v. Maine, 527 U.S. 706, 730 (1999). Furthermore, it is ironic that JUSTICE BREYER adopts such a textual approach in defending the conduct of an independent agency that itself lacks any textual basis in the Constitution.

indicating whether the Framers believed that the States' sovereign immunity would apply in such proceedings is unsurprising.

This Court, however, has applied a presumption—first explicitly stated in Hans v. Louisiana, supra—that the Constitution was not intended to "rais[e] up" any proceedings against the States that were "anomalous and unheard of when the Constitution was adopted." Id., at 18. We therefore attribute great significance to the fact that States were not subject to private suits in administrative adjudications at the time of the founding or for many years thereafter. For instance, while the United States asserts that "state entities have long been subject to similar administrative enforcement proceedings," Reply Brief for United States 12, the earliest example it provides did not occur until 1918, see id., at 14 (citing California Canneries Co. v. Southern Pacific Co., 51 I.C.C. 500 (1918)).

B

To decide whether the *Hans* presumption applies here, however, we must examine FMC adjudications to determine whether they are the type of proceedings from which the Framers would have thought the States possessed immunity when they agreed to enter the Union.

In another case asking whether an immunity present in the judicial context also applied to administrative adjudications, this Court considered whether administrative law judges share the same absolute immunity from suit as do Article III judges. See Butz v. Economou, 438 U.S. 478 (1978). Examining in that case the duties performed by an ALJ, this Court observed:

> "There can be little doubt that the role of the modern federal hearing examiner or administrative law judge ... is 'functionally comparable' to that of a judge. His powers are often, if not generally, comparable to those of a trial judge: He may issue subpoenas, rule on proffers of evidence, regulate the course of the hearing, and make or recommend decisions. More importantly, the process of agency adjudication is currently structured so as to assure that the hearing examiner exercises his independent judgment on the evidence before him, free from pressures by the parties or other officials within the agency." Id., at 513 (citation omitted).

Beyond the similarities between the role of an ALJ and that of a trial judge, this Court also noted the numerous common features shared by administrative adjudications and judicial proceedings:

> "[F]ederal administrative law requires that agency adjudication contain many of the same safeguards as are available in the judicial process. The proceedings are adversary in nature. They are conducted before a trier of fact insulated from political influence. A party is entitled to present his case by oral or documentary evidence, and the transcript of testimony and exhibits together with the pleadings consti-

tutes the exclusive record for decision. The parties are entitled to know the findings and conclusions on all of the issues of fact, law, or discretion presented on the record." Ibid. (citations omitted).

This Court therefore concluded in *Butz* that administrative law judges were "entitled to absolute immunity from damages liability for their judicial acts." Id., at 514.

Turning to FMC adjudications specifically, neither the Commission nor the United States disputes the Court of Appeals' characterization below that such a proceeding "walks, talks, and squawks very much like a lawsuit." 243 F.3d, at 174. Nor do they deny that the similarities identified in *Butz* between administrative adjudications and trial court proceedings are present here. See 46 CFR § 502.142 (2001).

A review of the FMC's Rules of Practice and Procedure confirms that FMC administrative proceedings bear a remarkably strong resemblance to civil litigation in federal courts. For example, the FMC's Rules governing pleadings are quite similar to those found in the Federal Rules of Civil Procedure. A case is commenced by the filing of a complaint.... The defendant then must file an answer, generally within 20 days of the date of service of the complaint, ... and may also file a motion to dismiss.... A defendant is also allowed to file counterclaims against the plaintiff.... If a defendant fails to respond to a complaint, default judgment may be entered on behalf of the plaintiff. Intervention is also allowed....

Likewise, discovery in FMC adjudications largely mirrors discovery in federal civil litigation.... In both types of proceedings, parties may conduct depositions, ... which are governed by similar requirements.... Parties may also discover evidence by: (1) serving written interrogatories ...; (2) requesting that another party either produce documents ... or allow entry on that party's property for the purpose of inspecting the property or designated objects thereon ...; and (3) submitting requests for admissions.... And a party failing to obey discovery orders in either type of proceeding is subject to a variety of sanctions, including the entry of default judgment....

Not only are discovery procedures virtually indistinguishable, but the role of the ALJ, the impartial officer designated to hear a case, see § 502.147, is similar to that of an Article III judge. An ALJ has the authority to "arrange and give notice of hearing." Ibid. At that hearing, he may

"prescribe the order in which evidence shall be presented; dispose of procedural requests or similar matters; hear and rule upon motions; administer oaths and affirmations; examine witnesses; direct witnesses to testify or produce evidence available to them which will aid in the determination of any question of fact in issue; rule upon offers of proof ... and dispose of any other matter that normally and properly arises in the course of proceedings." Ibid.

The ALJ also fixes "the time and manner of filing briefs," § 502.221(a), which contain findings of fact as well as legal argument. . . . After the submission of these briefs, the ALJ issues a decision that includes "a statement of findings and conclusions, as well as the reasons or basis therefor, upon all the material issues presented on the record, and the appropriate rule, order, section, relief, or denial thereof." § 502.223. Such relief may include an order directing the payment of reparations to an aggrieved party. . . . The ALJ's ruling subsequently becomes the final decision of the FMC unless a party, by filing exceptions, appeals to the Commission or the Commission decides to review the ALJ's decision "on its own initiative." § 502.227(a)(3). In cases where a complainant obtains reparations, an ALJ may also require the losing party to pay the prevailing party's attorney's fees. . . .

In short, the similarities between FMC proceedings and civil litigation are overwhelming. In fact, to the extent that situations arise in the course of FMC adjudications "which are not covered by a specific Commission rule," the FMC's own Rules of Practice and Procedure specifically provide that "the Federal Rules of Civil Procedure will be followed to the extent that they are consistent with sound administrative practice."[11] § 502.12.

C

The preeminent purpose of state sovereign immunity is to accord States the dignity that is consistent with their status as sovereign entities. See In re Ayers, 123 U.S. 443, 505 (1887). "The founding generation thought it 'neither becoming nor convenient that the several States of the Union, invested with that large residuum of sovereignty which had not been delegated to the United States, should be summoned as defendants to answer the complaints of private persons.'" Alden, 527 U.S., at 748 (quoting In re Ayers, supra, at 505, 8 S.Ct. 164).

Given both this interest in protecting States' dignity and the strong similarities between FMC proceedings and civil litigation, we hold that state sovereign immunity bars the FMC from adjudicating complaints filed by a private party against a nonconsenting State. Simply put, if the Framers thought it an impermissible affront to a State's dignity to be required to answer the complaints of private parties in federal courts, we cannot imagine that they would have found it acceptable to compel a State to do exactly the same thing before the administrative tribunal of an agency, such as the FMC. Cf. Alden, supra, at 749 ("Private suits against nonconsenting States . . . present 'the indignity of subjecting a State to the coercive process of judicial tribunals at the instance of private parties,' *regardless of the forum*") (quoting In re Ayers, supra, at 505) (citations

---

11. In addition, "[u]nless inconsistent with the requirements of the Administrative Procedure Act and [the FMC's Rules of Practice and Procedure], the Federal Rules of Evidence [are] applicable" in FMC adjudicative proceedings. 46 CFR § 502.156 (2001).

omitted; emphasis added). The affront to a State's dignity does not lessen when an adjudication takes place in an administrative tribunal as opposed to an Article III court.[12] In both instances, a State is required to defend itself in an adversarial proceeding against a private party before an impartial federal officer.[13] Moreover, it would be quite strange to prohibit Congress from exercising its Article I powers to abrogate state sovereign immunity in Article III judicial proceedings, see *Seminole Tribe*, 517 U.S., at 72, 116 S.Ct. 1114, but permit the use of those same Article I powers to create court-like administrative tribunals where sovereign immunity does not apply.[14]

D

The United States suggests two reasons why we should distinguish FMC administrative adjudications from judicial proceedings for purposes of state sovereign immunity. Both of these arguments are unavailing.

1

The United States first contends that sovereign immunity should not apply to FMC adjudications because the Commission's orders are not self-executing.... Whereas a court may enforce a judgment through the exercise of its contempt power, the FMC cannot enforce its own orders. Rather, the Commission's orders can only be enforced by a federal district court....

The United States presents a valid distinction between the authority possessed by the FMC and that of a court. For purposes of this case, however, it is a distinction without a meaningful difference. To the extent that the United States highlights this fact in order to suggest that a party alleged to have violated the Shipping Act is not coerced to participate in

---

12. One, in fact, could argue that allowing a private party to haul a State in front of such an administrative tribunal constitutes a greater insult to a State's dignity than requiring a State to appear in an Article III court presided over by a judge with life tenure nominated by the President of the United States and confirmed by the United States Senate.

13. Contrary to the suggestion contained in JUSTICE BREYER's dissenting opinion, our "basic analogy" is not "between a federal administrative proceeding triggered by a private citizen and a private citizen's lawsuit against a State" in a State's own courts. See post, at [55]. Rather, as our discussion above makes clear, the more apt comparison is between a complaint filed by a private party against a State with the

FMC and a lawsuit brought by a private party against a State in federal court.

14. While JUSTICE BREYER asserts by use of analogy that this case implicates the First Amendment right of citizens to petition the Federal Government for a redress of grievances, see post, at [55], the Constitution no more protects a citizen's right to litigate against a State in front of a federal administrative tribunal than it does a citizen's right to sue a State in federal court. Both types of proceedings were "anomalous and unheard of when the Constitution was adopted," Hans v. Louisiana, 134 U.S. 1, 18 (1890), and a private party plainly has no First Amendment right to haul a State in front of either an Article III court or a federal administrative tribunal.

FMC proceedings, it is mistaken. The relevant statutory scheme makes it quite clear that, absent sovereign immunity, States would effectively be required to defend themselves against private parties in front of the FMC.

A State seeking to contest the merits of a complaint filed against it by a private party must defend itself in front of the FMC or substantially compromise its ability to defend itself at all. For example, once the FMC issues a nonreparation order, and either the Attorney General or the injured private party seeks enforcement of that order in a federal district court,[15] the sanctioned party is *not* permitted to litigate the merits of its position in that court. See § 1713(c) (limiting district court review to whether the relevant order "was properly made and duly issued"). Moreover, if a party fails to appear before the FMC, it may not then argue the merits of its position in an appeal of the Commission's determination filed under 28 U.S.C. § 2342(3)(B)(iv). See United States v. L.A. Tucker Truck Lines, Inc., 344 U.S. 33, 37 (1952) ("Simple fairness to those who are engaged in the tasks of administration, and to litigants, requires as a general rule that courts should not topple over administrative decisions unless the administrative body not only has erred but has erred against objection made at the time appropriate under its practice").

Should a party choose to ignore an order issued by the FMC, the Commission may impose monetary penalties for each day of noncompliance. See 46 U.S.C.App. § 1712(a). The Commission may then request that the Attorney General of the United States seek to recover the amount assessed by the Commission in federal district court, see § 1712(e), and a State's sovereign immunity would not extend to that action, as it is one brought by the United States. Furthermore, once the FMC issues an order assessing a civil penalty, a sanctioned party may not later contest the merits of that order in an enforcement action brought by the Attorney General in federal district court. See ibid. (limiting review to whether the assessment of the civil penalty was "regularly made and duly issued"); United States v. Interlink Systems, Inc., 984 F.2d 79, 83 (C.A.2 1993) (holding that review of whether an order was "regularly made and duly issued" does not include review of the merits of the FMC's order).

Thus, any party, including a State, charged in a complaint by a private party with violating the Shipping Act is faced with the following options: appear before the Commission in a bid to persuade the FMC of the strength of its position or stand defenseless once enforcement of the Commission's nonreparation order or assessment of civil penalties is sought in federal district court.[16] To conclude that this choice does not coerce a State to

15. A reparation order issued by the FMC, by contrast, may be enforced in a United States district court only in an action brought by the injured private party. See Part IV–B, infra. 46 U.S.C.App. § 1713(d).

16. While JUSTICE BREYER argues that States' access to "full judicial review" of the Com-

mission's orders mitigates any coercion to participate in FMC adjudicative proceedings, post, at [58], he earlier concedes that a State must appear before the Commis-

participate in an FMC adjudication would be to blind ourselves to reality.[17]

The United States and JUSTICE BREYER maintain that any such coercion to participate in FMC proceedings is permissible because the States have consented to actions brought by the Federal Government. See *Alden,* 527 U.S., at 755–756 ("In ratifying the Constitution, the States consented to suits brought by . . . the Federal Government"). The Attorney General's decision to bring an enforcement action against a State after the conclusion of the Commission's proceedings, however, does not retroactively convert an FMC adjudication initiated and pursued by a private party into one initiated and pursued by the Federal Government. The prosecution of a complaint filed by a private party with the FMC is plainly not controlled by the United States, but rather is controlled by that private party; the only duty assumed by the FMC, and hence the United States, in conjunction with a private complaint is to assess its merits in an impartial manner. Indeed, the FMC does not even have the discretion to refuse to adjudicate complaints brought by private parties. See, e.g., 243 F.3d, at 176 ("The FMC had no choice but to adjudicate this dispute"). As a result, the United States plainly does not "exercise . . . political responsibility" for such complaints, but instead has impermissibly effected "a broad delegation to private persons to sue nonconsenting States."[18] *Alden,* supra, at 756.

2

The United States next suggests that sovereign immunity should not apply to FMC proceedings because they do not present the same threat to the financial integrity of States as do private judicial suits. The Government highlights the fact that, in contrast to a nonreparation order, for which the Attorney General may seek enforcement at the request of the Commission, a reparation order may be enforced in a United States district court only in an action brought by the private party to whom the award

---

sion in order "to obtain full judicial review of an adverse agency decision in a court of appeals," post, at [57]. This case therefore does not involve a situation where Congress has allowed a party to obtain full *de novo* judicial review of Commission orders without first appearing before the Commission, and we express no opinion as to whether sovereign immunity would apply to FMC adjudicative proceedings under such circumstances.

17. JUSTICE BREYER'S observation that private citizens may pressure the Federal Government in a variety of ways to take *other* actions that affect States is beside the point. See post, at [57–58]. Sovereign immunity concerns are not implicated, for example, when the Federal Government enacts a rule opposed by a State. See post,

at [58]. It is an entirely different matter, however, when the Federal Government attempts to coerce States into answering the complaints of private parties in an adjudicative proceeding. See Part III–C, supra.

18. Moreover, a State obviously will not know ex ante whether the Attorney General will choose to bring an enforcement action. Therefore, it is the mere prospect that he may do so that coerces a State to participate in FMC proceedings. For if a State does not present its arguments to the Commission, it will have all but lost any opportunity to defend itself in the event that the Attorney General later decides to seek enforcement of a Commission order or the Commission's assessment of civil penalties.

was made. See 46 U.S.C.App. § 1713(d)(1). The United States then points out that a State's sovereign immunity would extend to such a suit brought by a private party.

This argument, however, reflects a fundamental misunderstanding of the purposes of sovereign immunity. While state sovereign immunity serves the important function of shielding state treasuries and thus preserving "the States' ability to govern in accordance with the will of their citizens," *Alden*, supra, at 750–751, the doctrine's central purpose is to "accord the States the respect owed them as" joint sovereigns. See Puerto Rico Aqueduct and Sewer Authority v. Metcalf & Eddy, Inc., 506 U.S. 139, 146 (1993); see Part III–C, supra. It is for this reason, for instance, that sovereign immunity applies regardless of whether a private plaintiff's suit is for monetary damages or some other type of relief. See *Seminole Tribe,* 517 U.S., at 58 ("[W]e have often made it clear that the relief sought by a plaintiff suing a State is irrelevant to the question whether the suit is barred by the Eleventh Amendment").

Sovereign immunity does not merely constitute a defense to monetary liability or even to all types of liability. Rather, it provides an immunity from suit. The statutory scheme, as interpreted by the United States, is thus no more permissible than if Congress had allowed private parties to sue States in federal court for violations of the Shipping Act but precluded a court from awarding them any relief.

It is also worth noting that an FMC order that a State pay reparations to a private party may very well result in the withdrawal of funds from that State's treasury. A State subject to such an order at the conclusion of an FMC adjudicatory proceeding would either have to make the required payment to the injured private party or stand in violation of the Commission's order. If the State were willfully and knowingly to choose noncompliance, the Commission could assess a civil penalty of up to $25,000 a day against the State. See 46 U.S.C.App. § 1712(a). And if the State then refused to pay that penalty, the Attorney General, at the request of the Commission, could seek to recover that amount in a federal district court; because that action would be one brought by the Federal Government, the State's sovereign immunity would not extend to it.

To be sure, the United States suggests that the FMC's statutory authority to impose civil penalties for violations of reparation orders is "doubtful." Reply Brief for United States 7. The relevant statutory provisions, however, appear on their face to confer such authority. For while reparation orders and nonreparation orders are distinguished in other parts of the statutory scheme, see, e.g., 46 U.S.C.App. § 1713(c) and (d), the provision addressing civil penalties makes no such distinction. See § 1712(a). ("Whoever violates ... a Commission order is liable to the United States for a civil penalty"). The United States, moreover, does not even dispute that the FMC could impose a civil penalty on a State for failing to obey a nonreparation order, which, if enforced by the Attorney General, would also result in a levy upon that State's treasury.

IV

Two final arguments raised by the FMC and the United States remain to be addressed. Each is answered in part by reference to our decision in *Seminole Tribe*.

A

The FMC maintains that sovereign immunity should not bar the Commission from adjudicating Maritime Services' complaint because "[t]he constitutional necessity of uniformity in the regulation of maritime commerce limits the States' sovereignty with respect to the Federal Government's authority to regulate that commerce." Brief for Petitioner 29. This Court, however, has already held that the States' sovereign immunity extends to cases concerning maritime commerce. See, e.g., Ex parte New York, 256 U.S. 490 (1921). Moreover, *Seminole Tribe* precludes us from creating a new "maritime commerce" exception to state sovereign immunity. Although the Federal Government undoubtedly possesses an important interest in regulating maritime commerce, see U.S. Const., Art. I, § 8, cl. 3, we noted in *Seminole Tribe* that "the background principle of state sovereign immunity embodied in the Eleventh Amendment is not so ephemeral as to dissipate when the subject of the suit is an area ... that is under the exclusive control of the Federal Government,"[19] 517 U.S., at 72. Thus, "[e]ven when the Constitution vests in Congress complete lawmaking authority over a particular area, the Eleventh Amendment prevents congressional authorization of suits by private parties against unconsenting States." Ibid. Of course, the Federal Government retains ample means of ensuring that state-run ports comply with the Shipping Act and other valid federal rules governing ocean-borne commerce. The FMC, for example, remains free to investigate alleged violations of the Shipping Act, either upon its own initiative or upon information supplied by a private party, ... and to institute its own administrative proceeding against a state-run port.... Additionally, the Commission "may bring suit in a district court of the United States to enjoin conduct in violation of [the Act]." 46 U.S.C.App. § 1710(h)(1).[20] Indeed, the United States has advised us that

---

19. JUSTICE BREYER apparently does not accept this proposition, see post, at [54], maintaining that it is not supported by the text of the Tenth Amendment. The principle of state sovereign immunity enshrined in our constitutional framework, however, is not rooted in the Tenth Amendment. See Part II, supra. Moreover, to the extent that JUSTICE BREYER argues that the Federal Government's Article I power "[t]o regulate Commerce with foreign Nations, and among the several States," U.S. Const., Art. I, § 8, cl. 3, allows it to authorize private parties to sue nonconsenting States, see post, at [54], his quarrel is not with our decision today but with our decision in Seminole Tribe of Fla. v. Florida, 517 U.S. 44 (1996). See id., at 72.

20. For these reasons, private parties remain "perfectly free to complain to the Federal Government about unlawful State

the Court of Appeals' ruling below "should have little practical effect on the FMC's enforcement of the Shipping Act," Brief for United States in Opposition 20, and we have no reason to believe that our decision to affirm that judgment will lead to the parade of horribles envisioned by the FMC.

B

Finally, the United States maintains that even if sovereign immunity were to bar the FMC from adjudicating a private party's complaint against a state-run port for purposes of issuing a reparation order, the FMC should not be precluded from considering a private party's request for other forms of relief, such as a cease-and-desist order. . . . As we have previously noted, however, the primary function of sovereign immunity is not to protect State treasuries, see Part III–C, supra, but to afford the States the dignity and respect due sovereign entities. As a result, we explained in *Seminole Tribe* that "the relief sought by a plaintiff suing a State is irrelevant to the question whether the suit is barred by the Eleventh Amendment." 517 U.S., at 58. We see no reason why a different principle should apply in the realm of administrative adjudications.

* * *

While some might complain that our system of dual sovereignty is not a model of administrative convenience, see, e.g., post, at [59] (BREYER, J., dissenting), that is not its purpose. Rather, "[t]he 'constitutionally mandated balance of power' between the States and the Federal Government was adopted by the Framers to ensure the protection of 'our fundamental liberties.' " Atascadero State Hospital v. Scanlon, 473 U.S. 234, 242 (1985) (quoting Garcia v. San Antonio Metropolitan Transit Authority, 469 U.S. 528, 572 (1985) (Powell, J., dissenting)). By guarding against encroachments by the Federal Government on fundamental aspects of state sovereignty, such as sovereign immunity, we strive to maintain the balance of power embodied in our Constitution and thus to "reduce the risk of tyranny and abuse from either front." Gregory v. Ashcroft, 501 U.S., at 458. Although the Framers likely did not envision the intrusion on state sovereignty at issue in today's case, we are nonetheless confident that it is contrary to their constitutional design, and therefore affirm the judgment of the Court of Appeals.

It is so ordered.

■ JUSTICE STEVENS, dissenting.

JUSTICE BREYER has explained why the Court's recent sovereign immunity jurisprudence does not support today's decision. I join his opinion without reservation, but add these words to emphasize the weakness of the

---

activity" and "the Federal Government [remains] free to take subsequent legal action." Post, at [53] (BREYER, J., dissenting). The only step the FMC may not take, con-

sistent with this Court's sovereign immunity jurisprudence, is to adjudicate a dispute between a private party and a nonconsenting State.

two predicates for the majority's holding. Those predicates are, first, the Court's recent decision in Alden v. Maine, 527 U.S. 706 (1999), and second, the "preeminent" interest in according States the "dignity" that is their due. Ante, at [43].

Justice Souter has already demonstrated that *Alden's* creative "conception of state sovereign immunity . . . is true neither to history nor to the structure of the Constitution." 527 U.S., at 814 (dissenting opinion). And I have previously explained that the "dignity" rationale is " 'embarrassingly insufficient,' " Seminole Tribe of Fla. v. Florida, 517 U.S. 44 (1996) (dissenting opinion; citation omitted), in part because "Chief Justice Marshall early on laid to rest the view that the purpose of the Eleventh Amendment was to protect a State's dignity," id., at 96–97 (citing Cohens v. Virginia, 6 Wheat. [19 U.S.] 264, 406–407 (1821)).

This latter point is reinforced by the legislative history of the Eleventh Amendment. It is familiar learning that the Amendment was a response to this Court's decision in Chisholm v. Georgia, 2 Dall. [2 U.S.] 419 (1793). Less recognized, however, is that *Chisholm* necessarily decided two jurisdictional issues: that the Court had personal jurisdiction over the state defendant, and that it had subject-matter jurisdiction over the case.[21] The first proposed draft of a constitutional amendment responding to *Chisholm*—introduced in the House of Representatives in February, 1793, on the day after *Chisholm* was decided—would have overruled the first holding, but not the second.[22] That proposal was not adopted. Rather, a proposal introduced the following day in the Senate,[23] which was "cast in terms that we associate with subject matter jurisdiction,"[24] provided the basis for the present text of the Eleventh Amendment.

21. See Nelson, Sovereign Immunity as a Doctrine of Personal Jurisdiction, 115 Harv. L.Rev. 1561, 1565–1566 (2002).

22. The House proposal read: "[N]o state shall be liable to be made a party defendant, in any of the judicial courts, established, or which shall be established under the authority of the United States, at the suit of any person or persons, whether a citizen or citizens, or a foreigner or foreigners, or of any body politic or corporate, whether within or without the United States." Id., at 1602, and n. 211 (quoting Proceedings of the United States House of Representatives (Feb. 19, 1793), Gazette of the United States, Feb. 20, 1793, reprinted in 5 Documentary History of the Supreme Court of the United States, 1789–1800 pp. 605–606 (M. Marcus ed., 1994)) (internal quotation marks omitted).

23. The Senate proposal read: "The Judicial Power of the United States shall not extend to any Suits in Law or Equity commenced or prosecuted against any one of the United States by Citizens of another State or by Citizens or Subjects of any foreign State." Nelson, supra, at 1603, and n. 212 (quoting Resolution in the United States Senate (Feb. 20, 1793), reprinted in 5 Documentary History of the Supreme Court, supra, at 607–608) (internal quotation marks omitted). The Senate version closely tracked the ultimate language of the Eleventh Amendment. See U.S. Const., Amdt. 11 ("The Judicial power of the United States shall not be construed to extend to any suit in law or equity, commenced or prosecuted against one of the United States by Citizens of another State, or by Citizens or Subjects of any Foreign State").

24. Nelson, supra, at 1603.

This legislative history suggests that the Eleventh Amendment is best understood as having overruled *Chisholm's* subject-matter jurisdiction holding, thereby restricting the federal courts' diversity jurisdiction. However, the Amendment left intact *Chisholm's* personal jurisdiction holding: that the Constitution does not immunize States from a federal court's process. If the paramount concern of the Eleventh Amendment's framers had been protecting the so-called "dignity" interest of the States, surely Congress would have endorsed the first proposed amendment granting the States immunity from process, rather than the later proposal that merely delineates the subject matter jurisdiction of courts. Moreover, as Chief Justice Marshall recognized, a subject-matter reading of the Amendment makes sense, considering the states' interest in avoiding their creditors. See *Cohens v. Virginia,* 6 Wheat. [19 U.S.], at 406–407.

The reasons why the majority in *Chisholm* concluded that the "dignity" interests underlying the sovereign immunity of English Monarchs had not been inherited by the original 13 States remain valid today. See, e.g., *Seminole Tribe of Fla.,* 517 U.S., at 95–97 (STEVENS, J., dissenting). By extending the untethered "dignity" rationale to the context of routine federal administrative proceedings, today's decision is even more anachronistic than *Alden.*

■ JUSTICE BREYER, with whom JUSTICE STEVENS, JUSTICE SOUTER, and JUSTICE GINSBURG join, dissenting.

The Court holds that a private person cannot bring a complaint against a State to a federal administrative agency where the agency (1) will use an internal adjudicative process to decide if the complaint is well founded, and (2) if so, proceed to court to enforce the law. Where does the Constitution contain the principle of law that the Court enunciates? I cannot find the answer to this question in any text, in any tradition, or in any relevant purpose. In saying this, I do not simply reiterate the dissenting views set forth in many of the Court's recent sovereign immunity decisions. See, e.g., Kimel v. Florida Bd. of Regents, 528 U.S. 62 (2000); Alden v. Maine, 527 U.S. 706 (1999); College Savings Bank v. Florida Prepaid Postsecondary Ed. Expense Bd., 527 U.S. 666 (1999); Seminole Tribe of Fla. v. Florida, 517 U.S. 44 (1996). For even were I to believe that those decisions properly stated the law—which I do not—I still could not accept the Court's conclusion here.

I

At the outset one must understand the constitutional nature of the legal proceeding before us. The legal body conducting the proceeding, the Federal Maritime Commission, is an "independent" federal agency. Constitutionally speaking, an "independent" agency belongs neither to the Legislative Branch nor to the Judicial Branch of Government. Although Members of this Court have referred to agencies as a "fourth branch" of Government, FTC v. Ruberoid Co., 343 U.S. 470, 487 (1952) (Jackson, J., dissenting), the agencies, even "independent" agencies, are more appropriately considered to be part of the Executive Branch. See Freytag v. Commissioner, 501 U.S. 868, 910(1991) (SCALIA, J., concurring in part and concurring in judgment). The President appoints their chief administrators, typically a Chairman and Commissioners, subject to confirmation by the Senate. Cf. Bowsher v. Synar, 478 U.S. 714, 723 (1986). The agencies derive their legal powers from congressionally enacted statutes. And the agencies enforce those statutes, i.e., they "execute" them, in part by making rules or by adjudicating matters in dispute. Cf. Panama Refining Co. v. Ryan, 293 U.S. 388, 428–429 (1935).

The Court long ago laid to rest any constitutional doubts about whether the Constitution permitted Congress to delegate rulemaking and adjudicative powers to agencies.... That, in part, is because the Court established certain safeguards surrounding the exercise of these powers.... And the Court denied that those activities as safeguarded, however much they might *resemble* the activities of a legislature or court, fell within the scope of Article I or Article III of the Constitution.... Consequently, in exercising those powers, the agency is engaging in an Article II, Executive Branch activity. And the powers it is exercising are powers that the Executive Branch of Government must possess if it is to enforce modern law through administration.

This constitutional understanding explains why both commentators and courts have often attached the prefix "quasi" to descriptions of an agency's rulemaking or adjudicative functions.... The terms *"quasi* legislative" and *"quasi* adjudicative" indicate that the agency uses legislative *like* or court *like* procedures but that it is not, constitutionally speaking, either a legislature or a court....

The case before us presents a fairly typical example of a federal administrative agency's use of agency adjudication. Congress has enacted a statute, the Shipping Act of 1984 (Act or Shipping Act), 46 U.S.C.App. § 1701 et seq., which, among other things, forbids marine terminal operators to discriminate against terminal users. The Act grants the Federal Maritime Commission the authority to administer the Act. The law grants the Commission the authority to enforce the Act in a variety of ways, for example, by making rules and regulations, by issuing or revoking licenses, and by conducting investigations and issuing reports. It also permits a private person to file a complaint, which the Commission is to consider. Interestingly enough, it does not say that the Commission must determine the merits of the complaint through agency adjudication—though, for present purposes, I do not see that this statutory lacuna matters.

Regardless, the Federal Maritime Commission has decided to evaluate complaints through an adjudicative process. That process involves assignment to an administrative law judge, a hearing, an initial decision, Commission review, and a final Commission decision, followed by federal appellate court review, 28 U.S.C. § 2342(3)(B). The initial hearing, like a typical court hearing, involves a neutral decisionmaker, an opportunity to present a case or defense through oral or documentary evidence, a right to cross-examination and a written record that typically constitutes the basis for decision. But unlike a typical court proceeding, the agency process also may involve considerable hearsay, resolution of factual disputes through the use of "official notice," and final decisionmaking by a Commission that remains free to disregard the initial decision and decide the matter on its own—indeed through the application of substantive as well as procedural rules, that it, the Commission, itself has created....

The outcome of this process is often a Commission order, say an order that tells a party to cease and desist from certain activity or that tells one party to pay money damages (called "reparations") to another. The Commission cannot itself enforce such an order. Rather, the Shipping Act says that, to obtain enforcement of an order providing for money damages, the private party beneficiary of the order must obtain a court order. It adds that, to obtain enforcement of other commission orders, either the private party or the Attorney General must go to court. It also permits the Commission to seek a court injunction prohibiting any person from violating the Shipping Act. And it authorizes the Commission to assess civil penalties (payable to the United States) against a person who fails to obey a Commission order; but to collect the penalties, the Commission, again, must go to court.

The upshot is that this case involves a typical Executive Branch agency exercising typical Executive Branch powers seeking to determine whether a particular person has violated federal law.... The particular person in this instance is a state entity, the South Carolina State Ports Authority, and the agency is acting in response to the request of a private individual. But at first blush it is difficult to see why these special circumstances matter. After all, the Constitution created a Federal Government empowered to enact laws that would bind the States and it empowered that Federal Government to enforce those laws against the States. See Knickerbocker Ice Co. v. Stewart, 253 U.S. 149, 160 (1920). It also left private individuals perfectly free to complain to the Federal Government about unlawful state activity, and it left the Federal Government free to take subsequent legal action. Where then can the Court find its constitutional principle—the principle that the Constitution forbids an Executive Branch agency to determine through ordinary adjudicative processes whether such a private complaint is justified? As I have said, I cannot find that principle anywhere in the Constitution.

II

The Court's principle lacks any firm anchor in the Constitution's text. The Eleventh Amendment cannot help. It says:

"The *Judicial* power of the United States shall not ... extend to any suit ... commenced or

prosecuted against one of the ... States by Citizens of another State."
(Emphasis added.)

Federal administrative agencies do not exercise the "[j]udicial power of the
United States." ... Of course, this Court has read the words "Citizens of
another State" as if they also said "citizen of the same State." Hans v.
Louisiana, 134 U.S. 1 (1890). But it has never said that the words
"[j]udicial power of the United States" mean "the executive power of the
United States." Nor should it.

The Tenth Amendment cannot help. It says:

"The powers not delegated to the United States by the Constitution,
nor prohibited by it to the States, are reserved to the States respective-
ly, or to the people."

The Constitution has "delegated to the United States" the power here in
question, the power "[t]o regulate Commerce with foreign Nations, and
among the several States." U.S. Const., Art. I, § 8, cl. 3; see California v.
United States, 320 U.S. 577, 586 (1944). The Court finds within this
delegation a hidden reservation, a reservation that, due to sovereign
immunity, embodies the legal principle the Court enunciates. But the text
of the Tenth Amendment says nothing about any such hidden reservation,
one way or the other.

Indeed, the Court refers for textual support only to an earlier case,
namely Alden v. Maine, 527 U.S. 706 (1999) (holding that sovereign
immunity prohibits a private citizen from suing a State in state court), and,
through *Alden,* to the texts that *Alden* mentioned. These textual references
include: (1) what Alexander Hamilton described as a constitutional "postu-
late," namely that the States retain their immunity from "suits, without
their consent," unless there has been a "surrender" of that immunity "in
the plan of the convention," id., at 730 (internal quotation marks omitted);
(2) what the *Alden* majority called "the system of federalism established by
the Constitution," ibid.; and (3) what the *Alden* majority called "the
constitutional design," id., at 731. See also id., at 760–762 (SOUTER, J.,
dissenting) (noting that the Court's opinion nowhere relied on constitutional text).

Considered purely as constitutional text, these words—"constitutional
design," "system of federalism," and "plan of the convention"—suffer
several defects. Their language is highly abstract, making them difficult to
apply. They invite differing interpretations at least as much as do the
Constitution's own broad liberty-protecting phrases, such as "due process
of law" or the word "liberty" itself. And compared to these latter phrases,
they suffer the additional disadvantage that they do not actually appear
anywhere in the Constitution.... Regardless, unless supported by considerations of history, of constitutional purpose, or of related consequence,
those abstract phrases cannot support today's result.

54

III

Conceding that its conception of sovereign immunity is ungrounded in the Constitution's text, see ante, at [38–39], n. [19], the Court attempts to support its holding with history. But this effort is similarly destined to fail, because the very history to which the majority turned in *Alden* here argues against the Court's basic analogy—between a federal administrative proceeding triggered by a private citizen and a private citizen's lawsuit against a State.

In *Alden* the Court said that feudal law had created an 18th-century legal norm to the effect that " 'no lord could be sued by a vassal in his own court, but each petty lord was subject to suit in the courts of a higher lord.' " 527 U.S., at 741. It added that the Framers' silence about the matter had woven that feudal "norm" into the "constitutional design," i.e., had made it part of our "system of federalism" unchanged by the " 'plan of the convention.' " Id., at 714–717, 730, 740–743. And that norm, said the *Alden* Court, by analogy forbids a citizen ("vassal") to sue a State ("lord") in the "lord's" own courts. Here that same norm argues against immunity, for the forum at issue is federal—belonging by analogy to the "higher lord." And total 18th-century silence about state immunity in Article I proceedings would argue against, not in favor of, immunity.

In any event, the 18th century was not totally silent. The Framers enunciated in the "plan of the convention," the principle that the Federal Government may sue a State without its consent. See, e.g., West Virginia v. United States, 479 U.S. 305, 311 (1987). They also described in the First Amendment the right of a citizen to petition the Federal Government for a redress of grievances. See also United States v. Cruikshank, 92 U.S. 542, 552–553; cf. generally Mark, The Vestigial Constitution: The History and Significance of the Right to Petition, 66 Ford. L.Rev. 2153, 2227 (1998). The first principle applies here because only the Federal Government, not the private party, can—in light of this Court's recent sovereign immunity jurisprudence, see Seminole Tribe of Fla. v. Florida, 517 U.S. 44 (1996)— bring the ultimate court action necessary legally to force a State to comply with the relevant federal law. See supra, at [53]. The second principle applies here because a private citizen has asked the Federal Government to determine whether the State has complied with federal law and, if not, to take appropriate legal action in court.

Of course these two principles apply only through analogy. (The Court's decision also relies on analogy—one that jumps the separation-of-powers boundary that the Constitution establishes.) Yet the analogy seems apt. A private citizen, believing that a State has violated federal law, seeks a determination by an Executive Branch agency that he is right; the agency will make that determination through use of its own adjudicatory agency processes; and, if the State fails to comply, the Federal Government may bring an action against the State in federal court to enforce the federal law.

Twentieth-century legal history reinforces the appropriateness of this description. The growth of the administrative state has led this Court to determine that administrative agencies are not Article III courts, ... that they have broad discretion to proceed either through agency adjudication or through rulemaking, ... and that they may bring administrative enforcement proceedings against States. At a minimum these historically established legal principles argue strongly against any effort to analogize the present proceedings to a lawsuit brought by a private individual against a State in a state court or to an Eleventh Amendment type lawsuit brought by a private individual against a State in a federal court.

This is not to say that the analogy (with a citizen petitioning for federal intervention) is, historically speaking, a perfect one. As the Court points out, the Framers may not have "anticipated the vast growth of the administrative state," and the history of their debates "does not provide direct guidance." Ante, at [40]. But the Court is wrong to ignore the relevance and importance of what the Framers did say. And it is doubly wrong to attach "great" legal "significance" to the absence of 18th-and 19th-century administrative agency experience. See ante, at [41]. Even if those alive in the 18th century did not "anticipat[e] the vast growth of the administrative state," ante, at [40], they did write a Constitution designed to provide a framework for Government across the centuries, a framework that is flexible enough to meet modern needs. And we cannot read their silence about particular means as if it were an instruction to forbid their use.

IV

The Court argues that the basic purpose of "sovereign immunity" doctrine—namely preservation of a State's "dignity"—requires application of that doctrine here. It rests this argument upon (1) its efforts to analogize agency proceedings to court proceedings, and (2) its claim that the agency proceedings constitute a form of "compulsion" exercised by a private individual against the State. As I have just explained, I believe its efforts to analogize agencies to courts are, constitutionally speaking, too frail to support its conclusion. Neither can its claim of "compulsion" provide the necessary support.

Viewed from a purely legal perspective, the "compulsion" claim is far too weak. That is because the private individual lacks the legal authority to compel the State to comply with the law. For as I have noted, in light of the Court's recent sovereign immunity decisions, if an individual does bring suit to enforce the Commission's order, see 46 U.S.C.App. § 1713, the State would arguably be free to claim sovereign immunity. See *Seminole Tribe of Fla.,* supra. Only the Federal Government, acting through the Commission or the Attorney General, has the authority to compel the State to act.

In a typical instance, the private individual will file a complaint, the agency will adjudicate the complaint, and the agency will reach a decision. The State subsequently may take the matter to court in order to obtain judicial review of any adverse agency ruling, but, if it does so, its opponent in that court proceeding is *not* a private party, but the agency itself. 28 U.S.C. § 2344. (And unlike some other administrative schemes, see, e.g., Verizon Md., Inc. v. Public Serv. Comm'n of Md., 535 U.S. ___, ___, 122 S.Ct. 1753, 1763–1764, (2002) (SOUTER, J., concurring), the Commission would not be a party in name only.) Alternatively, the State may do nothing, in which case either the Commission or the Attorney General must seek a court order compelling the State to obey. 46 U.S.C.App. §§ 1710, 1713. The Commission, but not a private party, may assess a penalty against the State for noncompliance, § 1712; and only a court acting at the Commission's request can compel compliance with a penalty order. In sum, no one can legally compel the State's obedience to the Shipping Act's requirements without a court order, and in no case would a court issue such an order (absent a State's voluntary waiver of sovereign immunity, see Atascadero State Hospital v. Scanlon, 473 U.S. 234, 238 (1985)) absent the request of a federal agency or other federal instrumentality.

In *Alden* this Court distinguished for sovereign immunity purposes between (a) a lawsuit brought by the Federal Government and (b) a lawsuit brought by a private person. It held that principles of "sovereign immunity" barred suit in the latter instance but not the former, because the former—a suit by the Federal Government—"require[s] the exercise of political responsibility for each suit prosecuted against a State." 527 U.S., at 756. That same "exercise of political responsibility" must take place here in every instance prior to the issuance of an order that, from a legal perspective, will compel the State to obey. To repeat: Without a court proceeding the private individual cannot legally force the State to act, to pay, or to desist; only the Federal Government may institute a court proceeding; and, in deciding whether to do so, the Federal Government will exercise appropriate political responsibility. Cf. ibid.

Viewed from a practical perspective, the Court's "compulsion" claim proves far too much. Certainly, a private citizen's decision to file a complaint with the Commission can produce practical pressures upon the State to respond and eventually to comply with a Commission decision. By appearing before the Commission, the State will be able to obtain full judicial review of an adverse agency decision in a court of appeals (where it will face in opposition the Commission itself, not the private party). By appearing, the State will avoid any potential Commission-assessed monetary penalty. And by complying, it will avoid the adverse political, practical, and symbolic implications of being labeled a federal "lawbreaker."

Practical pressures such as these, however, cannot sufficiently "affront" a State's "dignity" as to warrant constitutional "sovereign immunity" protections, for it is easy to imagine comparable instances of clearly lawful private citizen complaints to Government that place a State under far greater practical pressures to comply. No one doubts, for example, that a private citizen can complain to Congress, which may threaten (should the

57

State fail to respond) to enact a new law that the State opposes. Nor does anyone deny that a private citizen, in complaining to a federal agency, may seek a rulemaking proceeding, which may lead the agency (should the State fail to respond) to enact a new agency rule that the State opposes. A private citizen may ask an agency formally to declare that a State is not in compliance with a statute or federal rule, even though from that formal declaration may flow a host of legal consequences adverse to a State's interests.... And one can easily imagine a legal scheme in which a private individual files a complaint like the one before us, but asks an agency staff member to investigate the matter, which investigation would lead to an order similar to the order at issue here with similar legal and practical consequences.

Viewed solely in terms of practical pressures, the pressures upon a State to respond before Congress or the agency, to answer the private citizen's accusations, to oppose his requests for legally adverse agency or congressional action, would seem no less powerful than those at issue here. Once one avoids the temptation to think (mistakenly) of an agency as a court, it is difficult to see why the practical pressures at issue here would "affront" a State's "dignity" any more than those just mentioned. And if the latter create no constitutional "dignity" problem, why should the former? The Court's answer—that "[s]overeign immunity concerns are not implicated" unless the "Federal Government attempts to coerce States into answering the complaints of private parties in an adjudicative proceeding," ante, at n. [___]—simply begs the question of *when* and *why* States should be entitled to special constitutional protection.

The Court's more direct response lies in its claim that the practical pressures here are special, arising from a set of statutes that deprive a nonresponding State of any meaningful judicial review of the agency's determinations. See ante, at [43–46]. The Court does not explain just what makes this kind of pressure constitutionally special. But in any event, the Court's response is inadequate. The statutes clearly provide the State with full judicial review of the initial agency decision should the State choose to seek that review. 28 U.S.C. § 2342(3)(B)(iv). That review cannot "affront" the State's "dignity, for it takes place in a court proceeding in which the Commission, not the private party, will oppose the State." § 2344.

Even were that not so, Congress could easily resolve the resulting problem by making clear that the relevant statutes authorize full judicial review in an enforcement action brought against a State. For that matter, one might interpret existing statutes as permitting in such actions whatever form of judicial review the Constitution demands. Cf. Crowell v. Benson, 285 U.S., at 45–47. Statutory language that authorizes review of whether an order was "properly made and duly issued," 46 U.S.C.App. § 1713(c), does not *forbid* review that the Constitution *requires*. But even were I to make the heroic assumption (which I do not believe) that this case implicates a reviewing court's statutory inability to apply constitutionally requisite standards of judicial review, I should still conclude that the Constitution permits the agency to consider the complaint here before us. The "review standards" problem concerns the later enforceability of the agency decision, and the Court must consider any such problem later in the context of a court order granting or denying review. Ashwander v. TVA, 297 U.S. 288, 347 (1936) (Brandeis, J., concurring) (" 'It is not the habit of the Court to decide questions of a constitutional nature unless absolutely necessary to a decision of the case' ").

V

The Court cannot justify today's decision in terms of its practical consequences. The decision, while permitting an agency to bring enforcement actions against States, forbids it to use agency adjudication in order to help decide whether to do so. Consequently the agency must rely more heavily upon its own informal staff investigations in order to decide whether a citizen's complaint has merit. The natural result is less agency flexibility, a larger federal bureaucracy, less fair procedure, and potentially less effective law enforcement.... And at least one of these consequences, the forced growth of unnecessary federal bureaucracy, undermines the very constitutional objectives the Court's decision claims to serve....

These consequences are not purely theoretical. The Court's decision may undermine enforcement against state employers of many laws designed to protect worker health and safety.... And it may inhibit the development of federal fair, rapid, and efficient, informal non-judicial responses to complaints, for example, of improper medical care (involving state hospitals). Cf. generally Macchiaroli, Medical Malpractice Screening Panels: Proposed Model Legislation to Cure Judicial Ills, 58 Geo. Wash. L.Rev. 181 (1990).

* * *

The Court's decision threatens to deny the Executive and Legislative Branches of Government the structural flexibility that the Constitution permits and which modern government demands. The Court derives from the abstract notion of state "dignity" a structural principle that limits the powers of both Congress and the President. Its reasoning rests almost exclusively upon the use of a formal analogy, which, as I have said, jumps ordinary separation-of-powers bounds. It places "great significance" upon the 18th-century absence of 20th-century administrative proceedings. See ante, at [41]. And its conclusion draws little support from considerations of constitutional purpose or related consequence. In its readiness to rest a structural limitation on so little evidence and in its willingness to interpret that limitation so broadly, the majority ignores a historical lesson, reflected in a constitutional understanding that the Court adopted long ago: An overly restrictive judicial interpretation of the Constitution's structural constraints (unlike its protections of certain basic liberties) will undermine the Constitution's own efforts to achieve its far more basic structural aim, the creation of a representative form of government capable of translating the people's will into effective public action.

This understanding, underlying constitutional interpretation since the New Deal, reflects the Constitution's demands for structural flexibility sufficient to adapt substantive laws and institutions to rapidly changing social, economic, and technological conditions. It reflects the comparative inability of the Judiciary to understand either those conditions or the need for new laws and new administrative forms they may create. It reflects the Framers' own aspiration to write a document that would "constitute" a democratic, liberty-protecting form of government that would endure through centuries of change. This understanding led the New Deal Court to reject overly restrictive formalistic interpretations of the Constitution's structural provisions, thereby permitting Congress to enact social and economic legislation that circumstances had led the public to demand. And it led that Court to find in the Constitution authorization for new forms of administration, including independent administrative agencies, with the legal authority flexibly to implement, *i.e.,* to "execute," through adjudication, through rulemaking, and in other ways, the legislation that Congress subsequently enacted. . . .

Where I believe the Court has departed from this basic understanding I have consistently dissented. . . . These decisions set loose an interpretive principle that restricts far too severely the authority of the Federal Government to regulate innumerable relationships between State and citizen. Just as this principle has no logical starting place, I fear that neither does it have any logical stopping point.

Today's decision reaffirms the need for continued dissent—unless the consequences of the Court's approach prove anodyne, as I hope, rather than randomly destructive, as I fear.

———

Lapides v. Board of Regents of the University System of Georgia

Supreme Court of the United States, 2002.
535 U.S. ___, 122 S.Ct. 1640, 152 L.Ed.2d 806.

■ JUSTICE BREYER delivered the opinion of the Court.

The Eleventh Amendment grants a State immunity from suit in federal court by citizens of other States, U.S. Const., Amdt. 11, and by its own citizens as well, Hans v. Louisiana, 134 U.S. 1 (1890). The question before us is whether the State's act of removing a lawsuit from state court to federal court waives this immunity. We hold that it does.

I

Paul Lapides, a professor employed by the Georgia state university system, brought this lawsuit in a Georgia state court. He sued respondents, the Board of Regents of the University System of Georgia (hereinafter Georgia or State) and university officials acting in both their personal capacities and as agents of the State. Lapides' lawsuit alleged that university officials placed allegations of sexual harassment in his personnel files. And Lapides claimed that their doing so violated both Georgia law, see Georgia Tort Claims Act, Ga.Code Ann. § 50–21–23 (1994) and federal law, see Civil Rights Act of 1871, Rev. Stat. § 1979, 42 U.S.C. § 1983.

All defendants joined in removing the case to Federal District Court, 28 U.S.C. § 1441, where they sought dismissal. Those individuals whom Lapides had sued in their personal capacities argued that the doctrine of "qualified immunity" barred Lapides' federal-law claims against them. And the District Court agreed. The State, while conceding that a state statute had waived sovereign immunity from state-law suits in state court, argued that, by virtue of the Eleventh Amendment, it remained immune from suit in federal court. See U.S. Const., Amdt. 11 (limiting scope of "judicial power of the *United States*" (emphasis added)). But the District Court did not agree. Rather, in its view, by removing the case from state to federal court, the State had waived its Eleventh Amendment immunity. See Atascadero State Hospital v. Scanlon, 473 U.S. 234, 238 (1985) (State may waive Eleventh Amendment immunity).

The State appealed the District Court's Eleventh Amendment ruling. See Puerto Rico Aqueduct and Sewer Authority v. Metcalf & Eddy, Inc., 506 U.S. 139, 144–145 (1993) (allowing interlocutory appeal). And the Court of Appeals for the Eleventh Circuit reversed. 251 F.3d 1372 (2001). In its view, state law was, at the least, unclear as to whether the State's attorney general possessed the legal authority to waive the State's Eleventh Amendment immunity. And, that being so, the State retained the legal right to assert its immunity, even after removal. See Ford Motor Co. v. Department of Treasury of Ind., 323 U.S. 459 (1945).

Lapides sought certiorari. We agreed to decide whether "a state waive[s] its Eleventh Amendment immunity by its affirmative litigation conduct when it removes a case to federal court...." Pet. for Cert. (i).

It has become clear that we must limit our answer to the context of state-law claims, in respect to which the State has explicitly waived immunity from state-court proceedings. That is because Lapides' only federal claim against the State arises under 42 U.S.C. § 1983, that claim seeks only monetary damages, and we have held that a State is not a "person" against whom a § 1983 claim for money damages might be asserted. Will v. Michigan Dept. of State Police, 491 U.S. 58, 66 (1989).... Hence this case does not present a valid federal claim against the State. Nor need we address the scope of waiver by removal in a situation where

61

the State's underlying sovereign immunity from suit has not been waived or abrogated in state court.

It has also become clear that, in the absence of any viable federal claim, the Federal District Court might well remand Lapides' state-law tort claims against the State to state court. 28 U.S.C. § 1367(c)(3). Nonetheless, Lapides' state-law tort claims against the State remain pending in Federal District Court, § 1367(a), and the law commits the remand question, ordinarily a matter of discretion, to the Federal District Court for decision in the first instance. . . . Hence, the question presented is not moot. We possess the legal power here to answer that question as limited to the state-law context just described. And, in light of differences of view among the lower courts, we shall do so. . . .

II

The Eleventh Amendment provides that the "Judicial power of the United States shall not be construed to extend to any suit . . . commenced or prosecuted against one of the . . . States" by citizens of another State, U.S. Const., Amdt. 11, and (as interpreted) by its own citizens. Hans v. Louisiana, 134 U.S. 1 (1890). A State remains free to waive its Eleventh Amendment immunity from suit in a federal court. See, e.g., *Atascadero*, supra, at 238. And the question before us now is whether a State waives that immunity when it removes a case from state court to federal court.

It would seem anomalous or inconsistent for a State both (1) to invoke federal jurisdiction, thereby contending that the "Judicial power of the United States" extends to the case at hand, and (2) to claim Eleventh Amendment immunity, thereby denying that the "Judicial power of the United States" extends to the case at hand. And a Constitution that permitted States to follow their litigation interests by freely asserting both claims in the same case could generate seriously unfair results. Thus, it is not surprising that more than a century ago this Court indicated that a State's voluntary appearance in federal court amounted to a waiver of its Eleventh Amendment immunity. Clark v. Barnard, 108 U.S. 436, 447 (1883) (State's "voluntary appearance" in federal court as an intervenor avoids Eleventh Amendment inquiry). The Court subsequently held, in the context of a bankruptcy claim, that a State "waives any immunity . . . respecting the adjudication of" a "claim" that it voluntarily files in federal court. Gardner v. New Jersey, 329 U.S. 565, 574 (1947). And the Court has made clear in general that "where a State *voluntarily* becomes a party to a cause and submits its rights for judicial determination, it will be bound thereby and cannot escape the result of its own voluntary act by invoking the prohibitions of the Eleventh Amendment." Gunter v. Atlantic Coast Line R. Co., 200 U.S. 273, 284 (1906) (emphasis added). The Court has long accepted this statement of the law as valid, often citing with approval the cases embodying that principle. . . .

In this case, the State was brought involuntarily into the case as a defendant in the original state-court proceedings. But the State then voluntarily agreed to remove the case to federal court. See 28 U.S.C. § 1446(a); Chicago, R.I. & P.R. Co. v. Martin, 178 U.S. 245, 248 (1900) (removal requires the consent of all defendants). In doing so, it voluntarily invoked the federal court's jurisdiction. And unless we are to abandon the general principle just stated, or unless there is something special about removal or about this case, the general legal principle requiring waiver ought to apply.

We see no reason to abandon the general principle. Georgia points out that the cases that stand for the principle, *Gunter, Gardner,* and *Clark,* did not involve suits for money damages against the State—the heart of the Eleventh Amendment's concern. But the principle enunciated in those cases did not turn upon the nature of the relief sought. And that principle remains sound as applied to suits for money damages.

Georgia adds that this Court decided *Gunter, Gardner,* and *Clark,* before it decided more recent cases, which have required a "clear" indication of the State's intent to waive its immunity. *College Savings Bank,* 527 U.S., at 675–681. But *College Savings Bank* distinguished the kind of constructive waivers repudiated there from waivers effected by litigation conduct. Id., at 681, n. 3. And this makes sense because an interpretation of the Eleventh Amendment that finds waiver in the litigation context rests upon the Amendment's presumed recognition of the judicial need to avoid inconsistency, anomaly, and unfairness, and not upon a State's actual preference or desire, which might, after all, favor selective use of "immunity" to achieve litigation advantages. See Wisconsin Dept. of Corrections v. Schacht, 524 U.S. 381, 393 (1998) (KENNEDY, J., concurring). The relevant "clarity" here must focus on the litigation act the State takes that creates the waiver. And that act—removal—is clear.

Nor has Georgia pointed to any special feature, either of removal or of this case, that would justify taking the case out from under the general rule. Georgia argues that its motive for removal was benign. It agreed to remove, not in order to obtain litigating advantages for itself, but to provide its co-defendants, the officials sued in their personal capacities, with the generous interlocutory appeal provisions available in federal, but not in state, court. Compare Mitchell v. Forsyth, 472 U.S. 511, 524–530 (1985) (authorizing interlocutory appeal of adverse qualified immunity determination), with Turner v. Giles, 264 Ga. 812, 813, 450 S.E.2d 421, 424 (1994) (limiting interlocutory appeals to those certified by trial court). And it intended, from the beginning, to return to state court, when and if its co-defendants had achieved their own legal victory.

A benign motive, however, cannot make the critical difference for which Georgia hopes. Motives are difficult to evaluate, while jurisdictional rules should be clear. See Hanover Star Milling Co. v. Metcalf, 240 U.S. 403, 426 (1916) (Holmes, J., concurring). To adopt the State's Eleventh

63

Amendment position would permit States to achieve "unfair tactical advantage[s,]" if not in this case, in others. See *Schacht,* supra, at 393–394, 398 (KENNEDY, J., concurring); cf. ALI, Study of the Division of Jurisdiction Between State and Federal Courts 366–367 (1968) (discussing the unfairness of allowing one who has invoked federal jurisdiction subsequently to challenge that jurisdiction). And that being so, the rationale for applying the general "voluntary invocation" principle is as strong here, in the context of removal, as elsewhere.

More importantly, Georgia argues that state law, while authorizing its attorney general "[t]o represent the state in all civil actions tried in any court," Ga.Code Ann. § 45–15–3(6) (1990); see Ga. Const., Art. 5, § 3, ¶ 4, does not authorize the attorney general to waive the State's Eleventh Amendment immunity.... Georgia adds that in *Ford,* 323 U.S. 459, this Court unanimously interpreted roughly similar state laws similarly, that the Court held that "no properly authorized executive or administrative officer of the state has waived the state's immunity," 323 U.S., at 469, and that it sustained an Eleventh Amendment defense raised for the first time after a State had litigated a claim brought against it in federal court and lost. That is to say, in *Ford* a State regained immunity by showing the attorney general's lack of statutory authority to waive—even after the State litigated and lost a case brought against it in federal court. Why, then, asks Georgia, can it not regain immunity in the same way, even after it removed its case to federal court?

The short answer to this question is that this case involves a State that *voluntarily* invoked the jurisdiction of the federal court, while *Ford* involved a State that a private plaintiff had *involuntarily* made a defendant in federal court. This Court consistently has found a waiver when a State's attorney general, authorized (as here) to bring a case in federal court, has voluntarily invoked that court's jurisdiction. See *Gardner,* 329 U.S., at 574–575; *Gunter,* 200 U.S., at 285–289, 292; cf. *Clark,* 108 U.S., at 447–448 (not inquiring into attorney general's authority). And the Eleventh Amendment waiver rules are different when a State's federal court participation is involuntary. See *Hans v. Louisiana,* 134 U.S. 1 (1890); cf. U.S. Const., Amdt. 11 (discussing suits "commenced or prosecuted against" a State).

But there is a more important answer. In large part the rule governing voluntary invocations of federal jurisdiction has rested upon the problems of inconsistency and unfairness that a contrary rule of law would create. *Gunter,* supra, at 284. And that determination reflects a belief that neither those who wrote the Eleventh Amendment nor the States themselves (insofar as they authorize litigation in federal courts) would intend to create that unfairness. As in analogous contexts, in which such matters are questions of federal law, cf., e.g., Regents of Univ. of Cal. v. Doe, 519 U.S. 425, 429, n. 5 (1997), whether a particular set of state laws, rules, or activities amounts to a waiver of the State's Eleventh Amendment immunity is a question of federal law. A rule of federal law that finds waiver through a state attorney general's invocation of federal-court jurisdiction avoids inconsistency and unfairness. A rule of federal law that, as in *Ford,* denies waiver despite the state attorney general's state-authorized litigating decision, does the opposite. For these reasons one Member of this Court has called for *Ford's* reexamination. *Schacht,* supra, at 394, 397 (KENNEDY, J., concurring). And for these same reasons, we conclude that *Clark, Gunter,* and *Gardner* represent the sounder line of authority. Finding *Ford* inconsistent with the basic rationale of that line of cases, we consequently overrule *Ford* insofar as it would otherwise apply.

The State makes several other arguments, none of which we find convincing. It points to cases in which this Court has permitted *the United States* to enter into a case voluntarily without giving up immunity or to assert immunity despite a previous effort to waive.... Those cases, however, do not involve the Eleventh Amendment—a specific text with a history that focuses upon the State's sovereignty vis-a-vis the Federal Government. And each case involves special circumstances not at issue here, for example, an effort by a sovereign (i.e., the United States) to seek the protection of its own courts (i.e., the federal courts), or an effort to protect an Indian tribe.

Finally, Georgia says that our conclusion will prove confusing, for States will have to guess what conduct might be deemed a waiver in order to avoid accidental waivers. But we believe the rule is a clear one, easily applied by both federal courts and the States themselves. It says that removal is a form of voluntary invocation of a federal court's jurisdiction sufficient to waive the State's otherwise valid objection to litigation of a matter (here of state law) in a federal forum. As Justice KENNEDY has pointed out, once "the States know or have reason to expect that removal will constitute a waiver, then it is easy enough to presume that an attorney authorized to represent the State can bind it to the jurisdiction of the federal court (for Eleventh Amendment purposes) by the consent to removal." See *Schacht,* 524 U.S., at 397 (concurring opinion).

We conclude that the State's action joining the removing of this case to federal court waived its Eleventh Amendment immunity—though, as we have said, the District Court may well find that this case, now raising only state-law issues, should nonetheless be remanded to the state courts for determination. 28 U.S.C. § 1367(c)(3).

For these reasons, the judgment of the Court of Appeals is reversed.

It is so ordered.

————

Verizon Maryland Inc. v. Public Service Commission of Maryland

Supreme Court of the United States, 2002.
536 U.S. ___, 122 S.Ct. 1753, ___ L.Ed.2d ___.

■ JUSTICE SCALIA delivered the opinion of the Court.

These cases present the question whether federal district courts have jurisdiction over a telecommunication carrier's claim that the order of a state utility commission requiring reciprocal compensation for telephone calls to Internet Service Providers violates federal law.

I

The Telecommunications Act of 1996 (1996 Act or Act), Pub.L. 104–104, 110 Stat. 56, created a new telecommunications regime designed to foster competition in local telephone markets. Toward that end, the Act imposed various obligations on incumbent local-exchange carriers (LECs), including a duty to share their networks with competitors. See 47 U.S.C. § 251(c). When a new entrant seeks access to a market, the incumbent LEC must "provide ... interconnection with" the incumbent's existing network, § 251(c)(2), and the carriers must then establish "reciprocal compensation arrangements" for transporting and terminating the calls placed by each others' customers, § 251(b)(5). As we have previously described, see AT & T Corp. v. Iowa Utilities Bd., 525 U.S. 366, 371–373 (1999), an incumbent LEC "may negotiate and enter into a binding agreement" with the new entrant "to fulfill the duties" imposed by §§ 251(b) and (c), but "without regard to the standards set forth" in those provisions. §§ 252(a)(1), 251(c)(1). That agreement must be submitted to the state commission for approval, § 252(e)(1), which may reject it if it discriminates against a carrier not a party or is not consistent with "the public interest, convenience, and necessity," § 252(e)(2)(A).

As required by the Act, the incumbent LEC in Maryland, petitioner Verizon Maryland Inc., formerly known as Bell Atlantic Maryland, Inc., negotiated an interconnection agreement with competitors, including MFS Intelenet of Maryland, later acquired by respondent MCI WorldCom, Inc. The Maryland Public Service Commission (Commission) approved the agreement. Six months later, Verizon informed WorldCom that it would no longer pay reciprocal compensation for telephone calls made by Verizon's customers to the local access numbers of Internet Service Providers (ISPs), claiming that ISP traffic was not "local traffic"[25] subject to the reciprocal compensation agreement because ISPs connect customers to distant Web sites. WorldCom disputed Verizon's claim and filed a complaint with the Commission. The Commission found in favor of WorldCom, ordering Veri-

---

25. Section 1.61 of the interconnection agreement provides: " 'Reciprocal Compensation' is As Described in the Act, and refers to the payment arrangements that recover costs incurred for the transport and termination of Local Traffic originating on one Party's network and terminating on the other Party's network." In turn, § 1.44 defines " 'Local Traffic' " as "traffic that is originated by a Customer of one Party on that Party's network and terminates to a Customer of the other Party on that other Party's network, within a given local calling area, or expanded area service ('EAS') area, as defined in [Bell Atlantic's] effective Customer tariffs. Local Traffic does not include traffic originated or terminated by a commercial mobile radio service carrier."

zon "to timely forward all future interconnection payments owed [World-Com] for telephone calls placed to an ISP" and to pay WorldCom any reciprocal compensation that it had withheld pending resolution of the dispute. Verizon appealed to a Maryland state court, which affirmed the order.

Subsequently, the Federal Communications Commission (FCC) issued a ruling—later vacated by the Court of Appeals for the D.C. Circuit, see Bell Atlantic Tel. Cos. v. FCC, 206 F.3d 1 (C.A.D.C.2000)—which categorized ISP-bound calls as nonlocal for purposes of reciprocal compensation but concluded that, absent a federal compensation mechanism for those calls, state commissions could construe interconnection agreements as requiring reciprocal compensation. Verizon filed a new complaint with the Commission, arguing that the FCC ruling established that Verizon was no longer required to provide reciprocal compensation for ISP traffic. In a 3–to–2 decision, the Commission rejected this contention, concluding that, as a matter of state contract law, WorldCom and Verizon had agreed to treat ISP-bound calls as local traffic subject to reciprocal compensation.

Verizon filed an action in the United States District Court for the District of Maryland, citing 47 U.S.C. § 252(e)(6) and 28 U.S.C. § 1331 as the basis for jurisdiction, and naming as defendants the Commission, its individual members in their official capacities, WorldCom, and other competing LECs. In its complaint, Verizon sought declaratory and injunctive relief from the Commission's order, alleging that the determination that Verizon must pay reciprocal compensation to WorldCom for ISP traffic violated the 1996 Act and the FCC ruling.

The District Court dismissed the action, and a divided panel of the Court of Appeals for the Fourth Circuit affirmed. 240 F.3d 279 (C.A.4 2001). The Fourth Circuit held that the Commission had not waived its immunity from suit by voluntarily participating in the regulatory scheme set up under the 1996 Act, and that the doctrine of Ex parte Young, 209 U.S. 123 (1908), does not permit suit against the individual commissioners in their official capacities. It then held that neither 47 U.S.C. § 252(e)(6) nor 28 U.S.C. § 1331 provides a basis for jurisdiction over Verizon's claims against the private defendants. Both Verizon and the United States, an intervenor below, petitioned this Court for review of the four questions resolved by the Fourth Circuit....

II

WorldCom, Verizon, and the United States contend that 47 U.S.C. § 252(e)(6) and 28 U.S.C. § 1331 independently grant federal courts subject-matter jurisdiction to determine whether the Commission's order requiring that Verizon pay WorldCom reciprocal compensation for ISP-bound calls violates the 1996 Act. Section 252 sets forth procedures relating to formation and commission approval of interconnection agreements, and commission approval and continuing review of interconnection terms and

67

conditions (called "[s]tatements of generally available terms," § 252(f)) filed by LECs. Section 252(e)(6) provides, in relevant part: "In any case in which a State commission makes a determination under this section, any party aggrieved by such determination may bring an action in an appropriate Federal district court to determine whether the agreement or statement meets the requirements of section 251 of this title and this section." The determination at issue here is neither the approval or disapproval of a negotiated agreement nor the approval or disapproval of a statement of generally available terms. WorldCom, Verizon, and the United States argue, however, that a state commission's authority under § 252 implicitly encompasses the authority to interpret and enforce an interconnection agreement that the commission has approved,[26] and that an interpretation or enforcement decision is therefore a "determination under [§ 252]" subject to federal review. Whether the text of § 252(e)(6) can be so construed is a question we need not decide. For we agree with the parties' alternative contention, that even if § 252(e)(6) does not *confer* jurisdiction, it at least does not *divest* the district courts of their authority under 28 U.S.C. § 1331 to review the Commission's order for compliance with federal law.

Verizon alleged in its complaint that the Commission violated the Act and the FCC ruling when it ordered payment of reciprocal compensation for ISP-bound calls. Verizon sought a declaratory judgment that the Commission's order was unlawful, and an injunction prohibiting its enforcement. We have no doubt that federal courts have jurisdiction under § 1331 to entertain such a suit. Verizon seeks relief from the Commission's order "on the ground that such regulation is pre-empted by a federal statute which, by virtue of the Supremacy Clause of the Constitution, must prevail," and its claim "thus presents a federal question which the federal courts have jurisdiction under 28 U.S.C. § 1331 to resolve." Shaw v. Delta Air Lines, Inc., 463 U.S. 85, 96, n. 14 (1983).[27]

The Commission contends that since the Act does not create a private cause of action to challenge the Commission's order, there is no jurisdiction to entertain such a suit. We need express no opinion on the premise of this argument. "It is firmly established in our cases that the absence of a valid (as opposed to arguable) cause of action does not implicate subject-matter jurisdiction, i.e., the court's statutory or constitutional *power* to adjudicate the case." Steel Co. v. Citizens for Better Environment, 523 U.S. 83, 89 (1998). As we have said, "the district court has jurisdiction if 'the right of the petitioners to recover under their complaint will be sustained if the

---

26. The Fourth Circuit suggested that both Maryland law and the Federal Communications Act of 1934 grant the Commission authority to interpret and enforce interconnection agreements that it approves under § 252.... The parties dispute whether it is in fact federal or state law that confers this authority, but no party contends that the Commission lacked jurisdiction to interpret and enforce the agreement.

27. [Footnote 14 from the Shaw case is reprinted in the main volume at p. 248, n. 8.]

Constitution and laws of the United States are given one construction and will be defeated if they are given another,' unless the claim 'clearly appears to be immaterial and made solely for the purpose of obtaining jurisdiction or where such a claim is wholly insubstantial and frivolous.' " Ibid. (citation omitted). Here, resolution of Verizon's claim turns on whether the Act, or an FCC ruling issued thereunder, precludes the Commission from ordering payment of reciprocal compensation, and there is no suggestion that Verizon's claim is " 'immaterial' " or " 'wholly insubstantial and frivolous.' " Ibid.

Verizon's claim thus falls within 28 U.S.C. § 1331's general grant of jurisdiction, and contrary to the Fourth Circuit's conclusion, nothing in 47 U.S.C. § 252(e)(6) purports to strip this jurisdiction. Section 252(e)(6) provides for federal review of an agreement when a state commission "makes a determination under [§ 252]." If this does not include (as WorldCom, Verizon, and the United States claim it does) the interpretation or enforcement of an interconnection agreement, then § 252(e)(6) merely makes *some other* actions by state commissions reviewable in federal court. This is not enough to eliminate jurisdiction under § 1331. Although the situation is not precisely parallel (in that here the elimination of federal district-court review would not amount to the elimination of all review), we think what we said in Abbott Laboratories v. Gardner, 387 U.S. 136, 141 (1967), is nonetheless apt: "The mere fact that some acts are made reviewable should not suffice to support an implication of exclusion as to others." (Internal quotation marks and citation omitted). And here there is nothing more than that mere fact. Section 252 does not establish a distinctive review mechanism for the commission actions that it covers (the mechanism is the same as § 1331: district-court review), and it does not distinctively limit the substantive relief available. Cf. United States v. Fausto, 484 U.S. 439, 448–449 (1988). Indeed, it does not even mention subject-matter jurisdiction, but reads like the conferral of a private right of action ("[A]ny party aggrieved by such determination may bring an action in an appropriate Federal district court," § 252(e)(6))....

And finally, none of the other provisions of the Act evince any intent to preclude federal review of a commission determination. If anything, they reinforce the conclusion that § 252(e)(6)'s silence on the subject leaves the jurisdictional grant of § 1331 untouched. For where otherwise applicable jurisdiction was meant to be excluded, it was excluded expressly. Section 252(e)(4) provides: "No State court shall have jurisdiction to review the action of a State commission in approving or rejecting an agreement under this section." In sum, nothing in the Act displays any intent to withdraw federal jurisdiction under § 1331; we will not presume that the statute means what it neither says nor fairly implies.[28]

---

28. The Commission also suggests that the *Rooker-Feldman* doctrine precludes a federal district court from exercising jurisdiction over Verizon's claim. See District of Columbia Court of Appeals v. Feldman, 460 U.S. 462 (1983); Rooker v. Fidelity Trust

III

The Commission nonetheless contends that the Eleventh Amendment bars Verizon's claim against it and its individual commissioners. World-Com, Verizon, and the United States counter that the Commission is subject to suit because it voluntarily participated in the regulatory regime established by the Act. Whether the Commission waived its immunity is another question we need not decide, because—as the same parties also argue—even absent waiver, Verizon may proceed against the individual commissioners in their official capacities, pursuant to the doctrine of Ex parte Young, 209 U.S. 123 (1908).

In determining whether the doctrine of Ex parte Young avoids an Eleventh Amendment bar to suit, a court need only conduct a "straightforward inquiry into whether [the] complaint alleges an ongoing violation of federal law and seeks relief properly characterized as prospective." Idaho v. Coeur d'Alene Tribe of Idaho, 521 U.S. 261, 296 (1997) (O'Connor, J., joined by Scalia and Thomas, JJ., concurring in part and concurring in judgment); see also id., at 298–299 (Souter, J., dissenting, joined by Stevens, Ginsburg, and Breyer, JJ.). Here Verizon sought injunctive and declaratory relief, alleging that the Commission's order requiring payment of reciprocal compensation was pre-empted by the 1996 Act and an FCC ruling. The prayer for injunctive relief—that state officials be restrained from enforcing an order in contravention of controlling federal law—clearly satisfies our "straightforward inquiry." We have approved injunction suits against state regulatory commissioners in like contexts. See, e.g., Prentis v. Atlantic Coast Line Co., 211 U.S. 210, 230 (1908) ("[W]hen the rate is fixed a bill against the commission to restrain the members from enforcing it will not be bad . . . as a suit against a State, and will be the proper form of remedy"); . . . Indeed, Ex parte Young itself was a suit against state officials (including state utility commissioners, though only the state attorney general appealed), to enjoin enforcement of a railroad commission's order requiring a reduction in rates. 209 U.S., at 129. As for Verizon's prayer for declaratory relief: That, to be sure, seeks a declaration of the *past,* as well as the *future,* ineffectiveness of the Commission's action, so that the past financial liability of private parties may be affected. But no past liability of the State, or of any of its commissioners, is at issue. It does not impose *upon the State* "a monetary loss resulting from a past breach of a legal duty on the part of the defendant state officials." Edelman v. Jordan, 415 U.S. 651, 668 (1974). Insofar as the exposure of the State is concerned, the prayer for declaratory relief adds nothing to the prayer for injunction.

Co., 263 U.S. 413 (1923). The *Rooker-Feldman* doctrine merely recognizes that 28 U.S.C. § 1331 is a grant of original jurisdiction, and does not authorize district courts to exercise appellate jurisdiction over state-court judgments, which Congress has reserved to this Court, see 28 U.S.C. § 1257(a). The doctrine has no application to judicial review of executive action, including determinations made by a state administrative agency.

The Fourth Circuit suggested that Verizon's claim could not be brought under Ex parte Young, because the Commission's order was probably *not* inconsistent with federal law after all. 240 F.3d, at 295–297. The court noted that the FCC ruling relied upon by Verizon does not seem to require compensation for ISP traffic; that the Court of Appeals for the D.C. Circuit has vacated the ruling; and that the Commission interpreted the interconnection agreement under state contract-law principles. It may (or may not) be true that the FCC's since-vacated ruling does not support Verizon's claim; it may (or may not) also be true that state contract law, and not federal law as Verizon contends, applies to disputes regarding the interpretation of Verizon's agreement. But the inquiry into whether suit lies under Ex parte Young does not include an analysis of the merits of the claim. See *Coeur d'Alene,* supra, at 281 ("An *allegation* of an ongoing violation of federal law ... is ordinarily sufficient" (emphasis added)).

Nor does the 1996 Act display any intent to foreclose jurisdiction under Ex parte Young—as we concluded the Indian Gaming Regulatory Act did in Seminole Tribe of Fla. v. Florida, 517 U.S. 44 (1996). There an Indian Tribe sued the State of Florida for violating a duty to negotiate imposed under that Act, 25 U.S.C. § 2710(d)(3). Congress had specified the means to enforce that duty in § 2710(d)(7), a provision "intended ... not only to define, but also to limit significantly, the duty imposed by § 2710(d)(3)." 517 U.S., at 74. The "intricate procedures set forth in that provision" prescribed that a court could issue an order directing the State to negotiate, that it could require the State to submit to mediation, and that it could order that the Secretary of the Interior be notified. Id., at 74–75. We concluded that "this quite modest set of sanctions" displayed an intent not to provide the "more complete and more immediate relief" that would otherwise be available under Ex parte Young. 517 U.S., at 75. Permitting suit under Ex parte Young was thus inconsistent with the "detailed remedial scheme," 517 U.S., at 74—and the limited one—that Congress had prescribed to enforce the State's statutory duty to negotiate. The Commission's argument that § 252(e)(6) constitutes a detailed and exclusive remedial scheme like the one in *Seminole Tribe,* implicitly excluding *Ex parte Young* actions, is without merit. That section provides only that when state commissions make certain "determinations," an aggrieved party may bring suit in federal court to establish compliance with the requirements of §§ 251 and 252. Even with regard to the "determinations" that it covers, it places no restriction on the relief a court can award. And it does not even say whom the suit is to be brought against—the state commission, the individual commissioners, or the carriers benefiting from the state commission's order. The mere fact that Congress has authorized federal courts to review whether the Commission's action complies with §§ 251 and 252 does not without more "impose upon the State a liability that is significantly more limited than would be the liability imposed upon the state officer under *Ex parte Young.*" *Seminole Tribe,* supra, at 75–76.

* * *

We conclude that 28 U.S.C. § 1331 provides a basis for jurisdiction over Verizon's claim that the Commission's order requiring reciprocal compensation for ISP-bound calls is pre-empted by federal law. We also conclude that the doctrine of Ex parte Young permits Verizon's suit to go forward against the state commissioners in their official capacities. We vacate the judgment of the Court of Appeals and remand these cases for further proceedings consistent with this opinion.

It is so ordered.

JUSTICE O'CONNOR took no part in the consideration or decision of these cases.

■ JUSTICE KENNEDY, concurring.

For the reasons well stated by the Court, I agree Verizon Maryland Inc. may proceed against the state commissioners in their official capacity under the doctrine of Ex parte Young, 209 U.S. 123 (1908). When the plaintiff seeks to enjoin a state utility commissioner from enforcing an order alleged to violate federal law, the Eleventh Amendment poses no bar. See Idaho v. Coeur d'Alene Tribe of Idaho, 521 U.S. 261, 271 (1997) (principal opinion of KENNEDY, J., joined by REHNQUIST, C. J.).

This is unlike the case in Idaho v. Coeur d'Alene Tribe of Idaho, supra, where the plaintiffs tried to use Ex parte Young to divest a State of sovereignty over territory within its boundaries. In such a case, a "straight-forward inquiry," which the Court endorses here, proves more complex. In *Coeur d'Alene* seven Members of this Court described Ex parte Young as requiring nothing more than an allegation of an ongoing violation of federal law and a request for prospective relief; they divided four to three, however, over whether that deceptively simple test had been met.

In my view, our *Ex parte Young* jurisprudence requires careful consideration of the sovereign interests of the State as well as the obligations of state officials to respect the supremacy of federal law. See *Coeur d'Alene,* supra, at 267–280 (principal opinion of KENNEDY, J., joined by REHNQUIST, C. J.). I believe this approach, whether stated in express terms or not, is the path followed in *Coeur d'Alene* as well as in the many cases preceding it. I also believe it necessary. Were it otherwise, the Eleventh Amendment, and not Ex parte Young, would become the legal fiction.

The complaint in this case, however, parallels the very suit permitted by Ex parte Young itself. With this brief explanation, I join the opinion of the Court.

■ JUSTICE SOUTER, with whom JUSTICE GINSBURG and JUSTICE BREYER join, concurring.

I join the Court's opinion, Part III of which rests on a ground all of us can agree upon:[29] on the assumption of an Eleventh Amendment bar, relief

---

29. In so doing, I set aside for the moment my continuing conviction that the interpre- tation of the Eleventh Amendment that a majority of this Court has embraced is funis available under the doctrine of *Ex parte Young,* 209 U.S. 123, 28 S.Ct. 441, 52 L.Ed. 714 (1908). Although that assumption apparently has been made from the start of the litigation, I think it is open to some doubt and so write separately to question whether these cases even implicate the Eleventh Amendment.

While the State of Maryland is the named defendant, it is only a nominal one. Verizon Maryland Inc., the private party "suing" it, does not seek money damages, or the sort of declaratory or injunctive relief that could be had against a private litigant.[30] Nor does Verizon seek an order enjoining the State from enforcing purely state-law rate orders of dubious constitutionality, the relief requested in Ex parte Young itself, 209 U.S., at 129–131. Instead, Verizon claims that the Maryland Public Service Commission has wrongly decided a question of federal law[31] under a decisional power conferred by the Telecommunications Act of 1996(Act), a power that no person may wield. Verizon accordingly seeks not a simple order of relief running against the state commission, but a different adjudication of a federal question by means of appellate review in Federal District Court,[32] whose jurisdiction to entertain the claim of error the Court today has affirmed. If the District Court should see things Verizon's way and reverse the state commission *qua* federal regulator, what dishonor would be done to the dignity of the State, which has accepted congressionally conferred power to decide matters of federal law in the first instance?

damentally mistaken. See Alden v. Maine, 527 U.S. 706, 760 (1999) (dissenting opinion); Seminole Tribe of Fla. v. Florida, 517 U.S. 44, 100 (1996) (dissenting opinion).

30. Compare, e.g., Board of Trustees of Univ. of Ala. v. Garrett, 531 U.S. 356, 360 (2001) (money damages from the State as employer under Title I of the Americans with Disabilities Act of 1990); Kimel v. Florida Bd. of Regents, 528 U.S. 62, 66 (2000) (money damages from the State as employer under the Age Discrimination in Employment Act of 1967); Alden v. Maine, supra, at 712 (money damages from the State as employer under the Fair Labor Standards Act of 1938 in state court); Florida Prepaid Postsecondary Ed. Expense Bd. v. College Savings Bank, 527 U.S. 627, 633 (1999) (money damages and injunctive and declaratory relief against a State for patent infringement); College Savings Bank v. Florida Prepaid Postsecondary Ed. Expense Bd., 527 U.S. 666, 671 (1999) (same for trademark violations); *Seminole Tribe,* supra, at 47 (suit to compel State to negotiate

in good faith); Hans v. Louisiana, 134 U.S. 1 (1890) (money damages for failure to honor state securities). In *Seminole Tribe,* a majority of this Court observed "that the relief sought by a plaintiff suing a State is irrelevant to the question whether the suit is barred by the Eleventh Amendment," 517 U.S., at 58, but this was said in the context of a suit for injunctive relief (to enforce a duty to negotiate) as opposed to money damages. My point is that conventional relief of both sorts (and declaratory relief) is different in kind from the judicial review of agency action sought in these cases.

31. Whether the interpretation of a reciprocal-compensation provision in a privately negotiated interconnection agreement presents a federal issue is a different question which neither the Court nor I address at the present.

32. Judicial review of FCC determinations under the Act is committed directly to the Courts of Appeal. 28 U.S.C. § 2342(1); 47 U.S.C. § 402(a).

One answer might be that even naming the state commission as a defendant in a suit for declaratory and injunctive relief in federal court is an unconstitutional indignity. But I do not see how this could be right. At least where the suit does not seek to bar a state authority from applying and enforcing state law, a request for declaratory or injunctive relief is simply a formality for obtaining a process of review. Cf. 4 K. Davis, Administrative Law Treatise 206 (2d ed. 1983) ("[T]he suit for injunction and declaratory judgment in a district court under 28 U.S.C. § 1331 ... is now always available to reach reviewable [federal] administrative action in absence of a specific statute making some other remedy exclusive"). And as for the nominal position of a State as defendant, "[i]t must be regarded as a settled doctrine of this court ... 'that the question whether a suit is within the prohibition of the 11th Amendment is not always determined by reference to the nominal parties on the record.' " In re Ayers, 123 U.S. 443, 487 (1887) (alteration in original) (quoting Poindexter v. Greenhow, 114 U.S. 270, 287 (1885)). If the applicability of the Eleventh Amendment pivots on the formalism that a State is found on the wrong side of the "v." in the case name of a regulatory appeal, constitutional immunity becomes nothing more than an accident of captioning practice in utility cases reviewed by courts. For that matter, the formal and nominal position of a governmental body in these circumstances is not even the universal practice. While the regulatory commission is generally a nominal defendant when a party appeals in the federal system, this is not the uniform practice among the States, several of which caption utility cases on judicial review in terms of the appealing utility.

The only credible response, which Maryland to its credit advances, is that the State has a strong interest in any case where its adjudication of a federal question is challenged. An adverse ruling in one appeal can no doubt affect the state commission's ruling in future cases. But this is true any time a state court decides a federal question and a successful appeal is made to this Court, and no one thinks that the Eleventh Amendment applies in that instance. See Cohens v. Virginia, 6 Wheat. [19 U.S.] 264, 412 (1821) (a writ of error from a state-court decision is not a "suit" under the Eleventh Amendment); McKesson Corp. v. Division of Alcoholic Beverages and Tobacco, Fla. Dept. of Business Regulation, 496 U.S. 18, 31 (1990) ("The Eleventh Amendment does not constrain the appellate jurisdiction of the Supreme Court over cases arising from state courts") (unanimous Court); cf. U.S. Const., Art. VI ("This Constitution, and the Laws of the United States ... shall be the supreme Law of the Land").[33] Whether an issue comes from a state-agency or a state-court decision, the federal court is reviewing the State's determination of a question of federal law, and it is neither prudent nor natural to see such review as impugning the dignity of the State or implicating the States' sovereign immunity in the federal system.

33. A possible ground for distinction is that the Supreme Court reviews state-court decisions while a Federal District Court initially reviews state-commission decisions under the Act. The argument would be that the Constitution requires any controversy in which a State's dignitary interests are implicated to be decided by this Court, and no other federal court, as a sign of respect for the State's sovereignty. See Farquhar v. Georgia (C.C. D.Ga.1791) (Iredell, J.), reprinted in 5 Documentary History of the Supreme Court of the United States, 1789–1800, pp. 148–154 (M. Marcus ed. 1994) ("It may also fairly be presumed that the several States thought it important to stipulate that so awful [and] important a Trial [to which a State is party] should not be cognizable in any Court but the Supreme"). But this position has long been rejected and is inconsistent with the doctrine of congressional abrogation, which presumes that States may be sued in federal District Court in the first instance when Congress properly so provides, see *Seminole Tribe,* 517 U.S., at 55.

SECTION 6. STATUTORY RESTRICTIONS ON ENJOINING STATE OFFICERS

Page 420. Add to Note 39.

The Civil Rights of Institutionalized Persons Act of 1980, 42 U.S.C. § 1997e, granted federal district judges discretionary powers to require a state prisoner to exhaust state administrative remedies before bringing a federal civil rights suit under 42 U.S.C. § 1983. This exhaustion requirement was stiffened and made mandatory to all suits by either state or federal prisoners "with respect to prison conditions" by the Prison Litigation Reform Act of 1995 (PLRA), 42 U.S.C. § 1997e(a). A unanimous Supreme Court adopted a very broad construction of "prison conditions" in Porter v. Nussle, 534 U.S. 516, ___, 122 S.Ct. 983, 992 (2002): "[T]he PLRA's exhaustion requirement applies to all inmate suits about prison life, whether they involve general circumstances or particular episodes, and whether they allege excessive force or some other wrong."

SECTION 7. THE ABSTENTION DOCTRINES

Page 434. Add to Footnote 47

In Johnson v. Collins Entertainment Co., Inc., 199 F.3d 710 (4th Cir.1999), the Fourth Circuit held that Burford abstention was required in a suit brought by habitual gamblers against the heavily regulated video-poker industry of South Carolina. The court was not deterred by two features of the suit generally deemed incompatible with Burford abstention: it involved federal-question rather than diversity jurisdiction, and sought damages as well as injunctive relief. In the latter respect the court bowed to Quackenbush by ordering a stay rather than dismissal of the damages claims, but also made it clear that the district court was to do nothing until the damages claims had been mooted by the parallel state proceedings necessitated by its dismissal of all claims for injunctive relief.

SECTION 8.   "OUR FEDERALISM"

Page 463. Insert in Footnote 58

The cross-reference to the Younger case should read "p. 457 supra".

SECTION 9.   HABEAS CORPUS

Page 498.

On the sixth line of this page, insert new footnote 88a at the end of the italicized text of 28 U.S.C. § 2244(b)(2)(A), after "unavailable;" and before "or".

[**88a.** In Tyler v. Cain, 533 U.S. 656, 121 S.Ct. 2478 (2001), a narrowly divided Court adopted a very strict construction of § 2244(b)(2)(A)'s exception permitting a second or successive application for a writ of habeas corpus grounded in a "new rule" that the Supreme Court has "made retroactive" for habeas purposes. Teague v. Lane, 489 U.S. 288 (1989), continues to govern whether a "new rule" *should* be "made" retroactive. Teague generally bars retroactive habeas application of new rules, subject to one substantive and one procedural exception: when (1) the new rule constitutionally decriminalizes "certain kinds of primary, private individual conduct" by placing them "beyond the power of the criminal law-making authority to proscribe"; or when (2) the new rule is a "watershed rule of criminal procedure" that is either closely tied either to "the likelihood of obtaining an accurate conviction" or to "bedrock procedural elements essential to the fairness of a proceeding." 489 U.S. at 311.]

Page 499.

In the fourth line from the bottom of this page, insert new footnote 88b at the end of the italicized text of 28 U.S.C. § 2244(d)(2).

[**88b.** If a "properly filed application for State post-conviction or other collateral review" is denied by an inferior state court, is the application "pending"—and the federal one-year limitations period accordingly tolled—during the period in which the denial of state habeas relief is subject to state appellate review? All members of the Court agreed that the federal period is tolled during throughout the appellate process, including the normally brief period between the denial of relief by a lower court and the prisoner's filing of a notice of appeal of that adverse ruling. But the Court fractured in applying this rule to California's unusual system of post-conviction appellate review, which permits a prisoner who has unsuccessfully sought habeas relief from a lower court to seek review of that adverse ruling either by appeal or by filing an independent but essentially identical petition for a writ of habeas corpus in a higher court. California prisoners typically choose the second option, and although the independent habeas petition must be filed in the appellate court within a "reasonable" time, unlike a notice of appeal it is not required to be filed within a determinate period. A narrow majority generously construed § 2244(d)(2) to toll the federal one-year limitations period throughout a gap of even several months between the denial of Saffold's habeas petition by a lower state court and the filing of an independent petition for habeas relief in the reviewing court, provided that on remand it was determined that this delay (which apparently resulted from the failure of the lower court to notify Saffold of its denial of his petition) was not "unreasonable" as a matter of state law. Carey v. Saffold, ___ U.S. ___, 122 S.Ct. 2134 (2002).]

Page 511.

Poker players will rejoice that the phrase "whole card" appearing in line 12 of the second full paragraph on page 511 of the main volume's reprinting of Wainwright v. Sykes—the phrase used in the slip opinion of the Supreme Court, and perpetuated in the Westlaw report of the case—was corrected in the final, bound version of the case in U.S. Reports to read "hole card".

Page 514. Add to Footnote 99

It was held in Edwards v. Carpenter, 529 U.S. 446 (2000), that ineffective assistance of counsel (IAC) is not "cause" excusing ineffective counsel's procedural default of an independent constitutional claim for federal habeas relief. Although counsel's procedural default forfeits the independent constitutional basis for relief from the underlying state-court conviction, the defendant may still seek federal habeas relief on IAC grounds.

Page 515. Substitute for Matteo v. Superintendent, SCI Albion

Williams v. Taylor

Supreme Court of the United States, (2000).
529 U.S. 362, 120 S.Ct. 1495, 146 L.Ed.2d 389.

■ JUSTICE STEVENS announced the judgment of the Court and delivered the opinion of the Court with respect to Parts, I, III, and IV, and an opinion with respect to Parts II and V.[6]

The questions presented are whether Terry Williams' constitutional right to the effective assistance of counsel as defined in Strickland v. Washington, 466 U.S. 668 (1984), was violated, and whether the judgment of the Virginia Supreme Court refusing to set aside his death sentence "was contrary to, or involved an unreasonable application of, clearly established Federal law, as determined by the Supreme Court of the United States," within the meaning of 28 U.S.C. § 2254(d)(1). We answer both questions affirmatively.

I

[Terry Williams was convicted and sentenced to death by a Virginia state court for the robbery and murder of Harris Stone, whose death had initially been attributed to blood-alcohol poisoning. Six months after Stone's death, while incarcerated for an unrelated offense, a remorseful Williams volunteered to the police that he had killed Stone and had taken from him "a few dollars" that Stone had refused to lend to Williams. He was convicted of robbery and capital murder on the basis of his confessions. At his sentencing hearing, the prosecution introduced evidence of two prior convictions and several instances of uncharged, violent criminal conduct, as

---

6.   JUSTICE SOUTER, JUSTICE GINSBURG, and JUSTICE BREYER join this opinion in its entirety. JUSTICE O'CONNOR and JUSTICE KENNEDY join Parts I, III, and IV of this opinion.

well as expert testimony that Williams would pose a serious, continuing threat to society. Williams' trial counsel offered a perfunctory and half-hearted defense at the sentencing hearing. The conviction and death sentence were upheld on direct review.]

State Habeas Corpus Proceedings

[In state habeas proceedings, postconviction counsel introduced substantial mitigating evidence that trial counsel had failed to present at the sentencing phase. The trial judge who had previously followed the jury's recommendation by sentencing Williams to death also presided over the state habeas hearing. The trial judge was persuaded that trial counsel's performance at the sentencing hearing had been so poor as to violate William's constitutional right to the effective assistance of counsel, and that Williams had been prejudiced by this violation. Acting as the state supreme court's special master, the trial judge recommended that Williams receive a rehearing of the penalty phase of his trial.]

The Virginia Supreme Court did not accept that recommendation. Williams v. Warden, 254 Va. 16, 487 S.E.2d 194 (1997). Although it assumed, without deciding, that trial counsel had been ineffective, id., at 23–26, 487 S.E.2d, at 198, 200, it disagreed with the trial judge's conclusion that Williams had suffered sufficient prejudice to warrant relief. Treating the prejudice inquiry as a mixed question of law and fact, the Virginia Supreme Court accepted the factual determination that available evidence in mitigation had not been presented at the trial, but held that the trial judge had misapplied the law in two respects. First, relying on our decision in Lockhart v. Fretwell, 506 U.S. 364 (1993), the court held that it was wrong for the trial judge to rely " 'on mere outcome determination' " when assessing prejudice, 254 Va., at 23, 487 S.E.2d, at 198 (quoting *Lockhart*, 506 U.S., at 369). Second, it construed the trial judge's opinion as having "adopted a per se approach" that would establish prejudice whenever any mitigating evidence was omitted. 254 Va., at 26, 487 S.E.2d, at 200.

The court then reviewed the prosecution evidence supporting the "future dangerousness" aggravating circumstance, reciting Williams' criminal history, including the several most recent offenses to which he had confessed. In comparison, it found that the excluded mitigating evidence—which it characterized as merely indicating "that numerous people, mostly relatives, thought that defendant was nonviolent and could cope very well in a structured environment," ibid.—"barely would have altered the profile of this defendant that was presented to the jury," ibid. On this basis, the court concluded that there was no reasonable possibility that the omitted evidence would have affected the jury's sentencing recommendation, and that Williams had failed to demonstrate that his sentencing proceeding was fundamentally unfair.

Federal Habeas Corpus Proceedings

Having exhausted his state remedies, Williams sought a federal writ of habeas corpus pursuant to 28 U.S.C. § 2254. After reviewing the state habeas hearing transcript and the state courts' findings of fact and conclusions of law, the federal trial judge agreed with the Virginia trial judge: The death sentence was constitutionally infirm.

After noting that the Virginia Supreme Court had not addressed the question whether trial counsel's performance at the sentencing hearing fell below the range of competence demanded of lawyers in criminal cases, the judge began by addressing that issue in detail. He identified five categories of mitigating evidence that counsel had failed to introduce, and he rejected the argument that counsel's failure to conduct an adequate investigation had been a strategic decision to rely almost entirely on the fact that Williams had voluntarily confessed.

. . . . .

Turning to the prejudice issue, the judge determined that there was " 'a reasonable probability that, but for counsel's unprofessional errors, the result of the proceeding would have been different.' *Strickland*, 466 U.S. at 694." He found that the Virginia Supreme Court had erroneously assumed that *Lockhart* had modified the *Strickland* standard for determining prejudice, and that it had made an important error of fact in discussing its finding of no prejudice.[7] Having introduced his analysis of Williams' claim with the standard of review applicable on habeas appeals provided by 28 U.S.C. § 2254(d), the judge concluded that those errors established that the Virginia Supreme Court's decision "was contrary to, or involved an unreasonable application of, clearly established Federal law" within the meaning of § 2254(d)(1).

The Federal Court of Appeals reversed. 163 F.3d 860 (C.A.4 1998). It construed § 2254(d)(1) as prohibiting the grant of habeas corpus relief unless the state court " 'decided the question by interpreting or applying the relevant precedent in a manner that reasonable jurists would all agree is unreasonable.' " Id., at 865 (quoting Green v. French, 143 F.3d 865, 870 (C.A.4 1998)). Applying that standard, it could not say that the Virginia Supreme Court's decision on the prejudice issue was an unreasonable application of the tests developed in either *Strickland* or *Lockhart*. It

---

7. "Specifically, the Virginia Supreme Court found no prejudice, reasoning: 'The mitigation evidence that the prisoner says, in retrospect, his trial counsel should have discovered and offered barely would have altered the profile of this defendant that was presented to the jury. At most, this evidence would have shown that numerous people, mostly relatives, thought that defendant was nonviolent and could cope very well in a structured environment.' The Virginia Supreme Court ignored or overlooked the evidence of Williams' difficult childhood and abuse and his limited mental capacity. It is also unreasonable to characterize the additional evidence as coming from 'mostly relatives.' As stated, Bruce Elliott, a respected professional in the community, and several correctional officers offered to testify on Williams' behalf."

explained that the evidence that Williams presented a future danger to society was "simply overwhelming," 163 F.3d, at 868, it endorsed the Virginia Supreme Court's interpretation of *Lockhart*, 163 F.3d, at 869, and it characterized the state court's understanding of the facts in this case as "reasonable," id., at 870.

We granted certiorari, 526 U.S. 1050 (1999), and now reverse.

II[8]

In 1867, Congress enacted a statute providing that federal courts "shall have power to grant writs of habeas corpus in all cases where any person may be restrained of his or her liberty in violation of the constitution, or of any treaty or law of the United States...." Act of Feb. 5, 1867, ch. 28, § 1, 14 Stat. 385. Over the years, the federal habeas corpus statute has been repeatedly amended, but the scope of that jurisdictional grant remains the same. It is, of course, well settled that the fact that constitutional error occurred in the proceedings that led to a state-court conviction may not alone be sufficient reason for concluding that a prisoner is entitled to the remedy of habeas. See, e.g., Stone v. Powell, 428 U.S. 465 (1976); Brecht v. Abrahamson, 507 U.S. 619 (1993). On the other hand, errors that undermine confidence in the fundamental fairness of the state adjudication certainly justify the issuance of the federal writ. See, e.g., Teague v. Lane, 489 U.S. 288, 311–314 (1989) (quoting Mackey v. United States, 401 U.S. 667, 692–694 (1971) (opinion of Harlan, J., concurring in judgments in part and dissenting in part), and quoting Rose v. Lundy, 455 U.S. 509, 544 (1982) (STEVENS, J., dissenting)). The deprivation of the right to the effective assistance of counsel recognized in *Strickland* is such an error. *Strickland*, 466 U.S., at 686, 697–698.

The warden here contends that federal habeas corpus relief is prohibited by the amendment to 28 U.S.C. § 2254, enacted as a part of the Antiterrorism and Effective Death Penalty Act of 1996 (AEDPA). The relevant portion of that amendment provides:

"(d) An application for a writ of habeas corpus on behalf of a person in custody pursuant to the judgment of a State court shall not be granted with respect to any claim that was adjudicated on the merits in State court proceedings unless the adjudication of the claim—

"(1) resulted in a decision that was contrary to, or involved an unreasonable application of, clearly established Federal law, as determined by the Supreme Court of the United States; ...."

In this case, the Court of Appeals applied the construction of the amendment that it had adopted in its earlier opinion in Green v. French,

[8. In Part II of his opinion, JUSTICE STEVENS wrote for only four Justices. Part II of JUSTICE O'CONNOR's opinion is the opinion of the Court with respect to the proper construction of 28 U.S.C. § 2254(d)(1).]

143 F.3d 865 (C.A.4 1998). It read the amendment as prohibiting federal courts from issuing the writ unless:

> "(a) the state court decision is in 'square conflict' with Supreme Court precedent that is controlling as to law and fact or (b) if no such controlling decision exists, 'the state court's resolution of a question of pure law rests upon an objectively unreasonable derivation of legal principles from the relevant [S]upreme [C]ourt precedents, or if its decision rests upon an objectively unreasonable application of established principles to new facts,' " 163 F.3d, at 865 (quoting *Green*, 143 F.3d, at 870).

Accordingly, it held that a federal court may issue habeas relief only if "the state courts have decided the question by interpreting or applying the relevant precedent in a manner that reasonable jurists would all agree is unreasonable," 163 F.3d, at 865.

We are convinced that that interpretation of the amendment is incorrect. It would impose a test for determining when a legal rule is clearly established that simply cannot be squared with the real practice of decisional law. It would apply a standard for determining the "reasonableness" of state-court decisions that is not contained in the statute itself, and that Congress surely did not intend. And it would wrongly require the federal courts, including this Court, to defer to state judges' interpretations of federal law.

As the Fourth Circuit would have it, a state-court judgment is "unreasonable" in the face of federal law only if all reasonable jurists would agree that the state court was unreasonable. Thus, in this case, for example, even if the Virginia Supreme Court misread our opinion in *Lockhart*, we could not grant relief unless we believed that none of the judges who agreed with the state court's interpretation of that case was a "reasonable jurist." But the statute says nothing about "reasonable judges," presumably because all, or virtually all, such judges occasionally commit error; they make decisions that in retrospect may be characterized as "unreasonable." Indeed, it is most unlikely that Congress would deliberately impose such a requirement of unanimity on federal judges. As Congress is acutely aware, reasonable lawyers and lawgivers regularly disagree with one another. Congress surely did not intend that the views of one such judge who might think that relief is not warranted in a particular case should always have greater weight than the contrary, considered judgment of several other reasonable judges.

The inquiry mandated by the amendment relates to the way in which a federal habeas court exercises its duty to decide constitutional questions; the amendment does not alter the underlying grant of jurisdiction in § 2254(a). . . . When federal judges exercise their federal-question jurisdiction under the "judicial Power" of Article III of the Constitution, it is "emphatically the province and duty" of those judges to "say what the law is." Marbury v. Madison, 1 Cranch [5 U.S.] 137, 177, 2 L.Ed. 60 (1803). At the core of this power is the federal courts' independent responsibility—independent from its coequal branches in the Federal Government, and independent from the separate authority of the several States—to interpret federal law. A construction of AEDPA that would require the federal courts to cede this authority to the courts of the States would be inconsistent with the practice that federal judges have traditionally followed in discharging their duties under Article III of the Constitution. If Congress had intended to require such an important change in the exercise of our jurisdiction, we believe it would have spoken with much greater clarity than is found in the text of AEDPA.

This basic premise informs our interpretation of both parts of § 2254(d)(1): first, the requirement that the determinations of state courts be tested only against "clearly established Federal law, as determined by the Supreme Court of the United States," and second, the prohibition on the issuance of the writ unless the state court's decision is "contrary to, or involved an unreasonable application of," that clearly established law. . . .

The "clearly established law" requirement

In Teague v. Lane, 489 U.S. 288 (1989), we held that the petitioner was not entitled to federal habeas relief because he was relying on a rule of federal law that had not been announced until after his state conviction became final. The antiretroactivity rule recognized in *Teague*, which prohibits reliance on "new rules," is the functional equivalent of a statutory provision commanding exclusive reliance on "clearly established law." Because there is no reason to believe that Congress intended to require federal courts to ask both whether a rule sought on habeas is "new" under *Teague*—which remains the law—and also whether it is "clearly established" under AEDPA, it seems safe to assume that Congress had congruent concepts in mind. It is perfectly clear that AEDPA codifies *Teague* to the extent that *Teague* requires federal habeas courts to deny relief that is contingent upon a rule of law not clearly established at the time the state conviction became final.[9]

9. We are not persuaded by the argument that because Congress used the words "clearly established law" and not "new rule," it meant in this section to codify an aspect of the doctrine of executive qualified immunity rather than *Teague*'s antiretroactivity bar. Brief for Respondent 28–29, n. 19. The warden refers us specifically to § 2244(b)(2)(A) and 28 U.S.C. § 2254(e)(2), in which the statute does in so many words employ the "new rule" language familiar to *Teague* and its progeny. Congress thus knew precisely the words to use if it had wished to codify *Teague* per se. That it did not use those words in § 2254(d) is evidence, the argu- ment goes, that it had something else in mind entirely in amending that section. We think, quite the contrary, that the verbatim adoption of the *Teague* language in these other sections bolsters our impression that Congress had *Teague*—and not any unrelated area of our jurisprudence— specifically in mind in amending the habeas statute. These provisions, seen together, make it impossible to conclude that Congress was not fully aware of, and interested in codifying into law, that aspect of this Court's habeas doctrine. We will not assume that in a single subsection of an amendment entirely devoted to the law of

Teague's core principles are therefore relevant to our construction of this requirement. Justice Harlan recognized the "inevitable difficulties" that come with "attempting 'to determine whether a particular decision has really announced a "new" rule at all or whether it has simply applied a well-established constitutional principle to govern a case which is closely analogous to those which have been previously considered in the prior case law.'" *Mackey*, 401 U.S., at 695 (quoting Desist v. United States, 394 U.S. 244, 263 (1969)). But *Teague* established some guidance for making this determination, explaining that a federal habeas court operates within the bounds of comity and finality if it applies a rule "dictated by precedent existing at the time the defendant's conviction became final." *Teague*, 489 U.S., at 301 (emphasis deleted). A rule that "breaks new ground or imposes a new obligation on the States or the Federal Government," ibid., falls outside this universe of federal law.

To this, AEDPA has added, immediately following the "clearly established law" requirement, a clause limiting the area of relevant law to that "determined by the Supreme Court of the United States." 28 U.S.C. § 2254(d)(1). If this Court has not broken sufficient legal ground to establish an asked-for constitutional principle, the lower federal courts cannot themselves establish such a principle with clarity sufficient to satisfy the AEDPA bar. In this respect, we agree with the Seventh Circuit that this clause "extends the principle of *Teague* by limiting the source of doctrine on which a federal court may rely in addressing the application for a writ." Lindh v. Murphy, 96 F.3d 856, 869 (C.A.7 1996)....

A rule that fails to satisfy the foregoing criteria is barred by *Teague* from application on collateral review, and, similarly, is not available as a basis for relief in a habeas case to which AEDPA applies.

. . . . .

The "contrary to, or an unreasonable application of," requirement

The message that Congress intended to convey by using the phrases, "contrary to" and "unreasonable application of" is not entirely clear. The prevailing view in the Circuits is that the former phrase requires de novo review of "pure" questions of law and the latter requires some sort of "reasonability" review of so-called mixed questions of law and fact....

We are not persuaded that the phrases define two mutually exclusive categories of questions. Most constitutional questions that arise in habeas corpus proceedings—and therefore most "decisions" to be made—require the federal judge to apply a rule of law to a set of facts, some of which may be disputed and some undisputed. For example, an erroneous conclusion that particular circumstances established the voluntariness of a confession,

habeas corpus, Congress made the anomalous choice of reaching into the doctrinally distinct law of qualified immunity, for a single phrase that just so happens to be the conceptual twin of a dominant principle in habeas law of which Congress was fully aware.

or that there exists a conflict of interest when one attorney represents multiple defendants, may well be described either as "contrary to" or as an "unreasonable application of" the governing rule of law. . . . In constitutional adjudication, as in the common law, rules of law often develop incrementally as earlier decisions are applied to new factual situations. . . . But rules that depend upon such elaboration are hardly less lawlike than those that establish a bright-line test.

.   .   .   .   .

. . . Whether or not a federal court can issue the writ under the "unreasonable application" clause, the statute is clear that habeas may issue under § 2254(d)(1) if a state court "decision" is "contrary to . . . clearly established Federal law." We thus anticipate that there will be a variety of cases, like this one, in which both phrases may be implicated.

Even though we cannot conclude that the phrases establish "a body of rigid rules," they do express a "mood" that the federal judiciary must respect. Universal Camera Corp. v. NLRB, 340 U.S. 474, 487 (1951). In this respect, it seems clear that Congress intended federal judges to attend with the utmost care to state-court decisions, including all of the reasons supporting their decisions, before concluding that those proceedings were infected by constitutional error sufficiently serious to warrant the issuance of the writ. Likewise, the statute in a separate provision provides for the habeas remedy when a state-court decision "was based on an unreasonable determination of the facts *in light of the evidence presented in the State court proceeding.*" 28 U.S.C. § 2254(d)(2) (emphasis added). While this provision is not before us in this case, it provides relevant context for our interpretation of § 2254(d)(1); in this respect, it bolsters our conviction that federal habeas courts must take as the starting point of their analysis the state courts' determinations of fact, including that aspect of a "mixed question" that rests on a finding of fact. AEDPA plainly sought to ensure a level of "deference to the determinations of state courts," provided those determinations did not conflict with federal law or apply federal law in an unreasonable way. H.R. Conf. Rep. No. 104–518, p. 111 (1996). Congress wished to curb delays, to prevent "retrials" on federal habeas, and to give effect to state convictions to the extent possible under law. When federal courts are able to fulfill these goals within the bounds of the law, AEDPA instructs them to do so.

.   .   .   .   .

Our disagreement with JUSTICE O'CONNOR about the precise meaning of the phrase "contrary to," and the word "unreasonable," is, of course, important, but should affect only a narrow category of cases. The simplest and first definition of "contrary to" as a phrase is "in conflict with." Webster's Ninth New Collegiate Dictionary 285 (1983). In this sense, we think the phrase surely capacious enough to include a finding that the state-court "decision" is simply "erroneous" or wrong. . . . Moreover, state-court decisions that do not "conflict" with federal law will rarely be "unreasonable" under either her reading of the statute or ours. We all agree that state-court judgments must be upheld unless, after the closest examination of the state-court judgment, a federal court is firmly convinced that a federal constitutional right has been violated. Our difference is as to the cases in which, at first-blush, a state-court judgment seems entirely reasonable, but thorough analysis by a federal court produces a firm conviction that that judgment is infected by constitutional error. In our view, such an erroneous judgment is "unreasonable" within the meaning of the act even though that conclusion was not immediately apparent.

In sum, the statute directs federal courts to attend to every state-court judgment with utmost care, but it does not require them to defer to the opinion of every reasonable state-court judge on the content of federal law. If, after carefully weighing all the reasons for accepting a state court's judgment, a federal court is convinced that a prisoner's custody—or, as in this case, his sentence of death—violates the Constitution, that independent judgment should prevail. Otherwise the federal "law as determined by the Supreme Court of the United States" might be applied by the federal courts one way in Virginia and another way in California. In light of the well-recognized interest in ensuring that federal courts interpret federal law in a uniform way, we are convinced that Congress did not intend the statute to produce such a result.

III

In this case, Williams contends that he was denied his constitutionally guaranteed right to the effective assistance of counsel when his trial lawyers failed to investigate and to present substantial mitigating evidence to the sentencing jury. The threshold question under AEDPA is whether Williams seeks to apply a rule of law that was clearly established at the time his state-court conviction became final. That question is easily answered because the merits of his claim are squarely governed by our holding in Strickland v. Washington, 466 U.S. 668 (1984).

.   .   .   .   .

It is past question that the rule set forth in *Strickland* qualifies as "clearly established Federal law, as determined by the Supreme Court of the United States." ... Williams is therefore entitled to relief if the Virginia Supreme Court's decision rejecting his ineffective-assistance claim was either "contrary to, or involved an unreasonable application of," that established law. It was both.

IV

The Virginia Supreme Court erred in holding that our decision in Lockhart v. Fretwell, 506 U.S. 364 (1993), modified or in some way supplanted the rule set down in *Strickland*....

.   .   .   .   .

85

V

In our judgment, the state trial judge was correct both in his recognition of the established legal standard for determining counsel's effectiveness, and in his conclusion that the entire postconviction record, viewed as a whole and cumulative of mitigation evidence presented originally, raised "a reasonable probability that the result of the sentencing proceeding would have been different" if competent counsel had presented and explained the significance of all the available evidence. It follows that the Virginia Supreme Court rendered a "decision that was contrary to, or involved an unreasonable application of, clearly established Federal law." Williams' constitutional right to the effective assistance of counsel as defined in Strickland v. Washington, 466 U.S. 668 (1984), was violated.

Accordingly, the judgment of the Court of Appeals is reversed, and the case is remanded for further proceedings consistent with this opinion.

It is so ordered.

■ JUSTICE O'CONNOR delivered the opinion of the Court with respect to Part II (except as to the footnote), concurred in part, and concurred in the judgment.[10]

In 1996, Congress enacted the Antiterrorism and Effective Death Penalty Act (AEDPA). In that Act, Congress placed a new restriction on the power of federal courts to grant writs of habeas corpus to state prisoners. The relevant provision, 28 U.S.C. § 2254(d)(1), prohibits a federal court from granting an application for a writ of habeas corpus with respect to a claim adjudicated on the merits in state court unless that adjudication "resulted in a decision that was contrary to, or involved an unreasonable application of, clearly established Federal law, as determined by the Supreme Court of the United States." The Court holds today that the Virginia Supreme Court's adjudication of Terry Williams' application for state habeas corpus relief resulted in just such a decision. I agree with that determination and join Parts I, III, and IV of the Court's opinion. Because I disagree, however, with the interpretation of § 2254(d)(1) set forth in Part II of JUSTICE STEVENS' opinion, I write separately to explain my views.

I

Before 1996, this Court held that a federal court entertaining a state prisoner's application for habeas relief must exercise its independent judgment when deciding both questions of constitutional law and mixed constitutional questions (i.e., application of constitutional law to fact). See, e.g., Miller v. Fenton, 474 U.S. 104, 112 (1985). In other words, a federal habeas

---

10. JUSTICE KENNEDY joins this opinion in its entirety. THE CHIEF JUSTICE and JUSTICE THOMAS join this opinion with respect to Part II. JUSTICE SCALIA joins this opinion with respect to Part II, except as to the footnote, infra [11].

court owed no deference to a state court's resolution of such questions of law or mixed questions....

. . . . .

If today's case were governed by the federal habeas statute prior to Congress' enactment of AEDPA in 1996, I would agree with JUSTICE STEVENS that Williams' petition for habeas relief must be granted if we, in our independent judgment, were to conclude that his Sixth Amendment right to effective assistance of counsel was violated. See ante, at [85].

II

A

Williams' case is *not* governed by the pre–1996 version of the habeas statute. Because he filed his petition in December 1997, Williams' case is governed by the statute as amended by AEDPA. Section 2254 now provides:

"(d) An application for a writ of habeas corpus on behalf of a person in custody pursuant to the judgment of a State court shall not be granted with respect to any claim that was adjudicated on the merits in State court proceedings unless the adjudication of the claim—

"(1) resulted in a decision that was contrary to, or involved an unreasonable application of, clearly established Federal law, as determined by the Supreme Court of the United States."

Accordingly, for Williams to obtain federal habeas relief, he must first demonstrate that his case satisfies the condition set by § 2254(d)(1). That provision modifies the role of federal habeas courts in reviewing petitions filed by state prisoners.

JUSTICE STEVENS' opinion in Part II essentially contends that § 2254(d)(1) does not alter the previously settled rule of independent review....

. . . . .

JUSTICE STEVENS arrives at his erroneous interpretation by means of one critical misstep. He fails to give independent meaning to both the "contrary to" and "unreasonable application" clauses of the statute.... By reading § 2254(d)(1) as one general restriction on the power of the federal habeas court, JUSTICE STEVENS manages to avoid confronting the specific meaning of the statute's "unreasonable application" clause and its ramifications for the independent-review rule. It is, however, a cardinal principle of statutory construction that we must " 'give effect, if possible, to every clause and word of a statute.' " ... Section 2254(d)(1) defines two categories of cases in which a state prisoner may obtain federal habeas relief with respect to a claim adjudicated on the merits in state court. Under the statute, a federal court may grant a writ of habeas corpus if the relevant state-court decision was either (1) "*contrary to* ... clearly established Federal law, as determined by the Supreme Court of the United States," or (2) "*involved an unreasonable application of* . . . clearly established Federal law, as determined by the Supreme Court of the United States." (Emphases added.)

The Court of Appeals for the Fourth Circuit properly accorded both the "contrary to" and "unreasonable application" clauses independent meaning. The Fourth Circuit's interpretation of § 2254(d)(1) in Williams' case relied, in turn, on that court's previous decision in Green v. French, 143 F.3d 865 (1998), cert. denied, 525 U.S. 1090 (1999). . . . With respect to the first of the two statutory clauses, the Fourth Circuit held in *Green* that a state-court decision can be "contrary to" this Court's clearly established precedent in two ways. First, a state-court decision is contrary to this Court's precedent if the state court arrives at a conclusion opposite to that reached by this Court on a question of law. Second, a state-court decision is also contrary to this Court's precedent if the state court confronts facts that are materially indistinguishable from a relevant Supreme Court precedent and arrives at a result opposite to ours. See 143 F.3d, at 869–870.

The word "contrary" is commonly understood to mean "diametrically different," "opposite in character or nature," or "mutually opposed." Webster's Third New International Dictionary 495 (1976). The text of § 2254(d)(1) therefore suggests that the state court's decision must be substantially different from the relevant precedent of this Court. The Fourth Circuit's interpretation of the "contrary to" clause accurately reflects this textual meaning. A state-court decision will certainly be contrary to our clearly established precedent if the state court applies a rule that contradicts the governing law set forth in our cases. Take, for example, our decision in Strickland v. Washington, 466 U.S. 668 (1984). If a state court were to reject a prisoner's claim of ineffective assistance of counsel on the grounds that the prisoner had not established by a preponderance of the evidence that the result of his criminal proceeding would have been different, that decision would be "diametrically different," "opposite in character or nature," and "mutually opposed" to our clearly established precedent because we held in *Strickland* that the prisoner need only demonstrate a "reasonable probability that . . . the result of the proceeding would have been different." Id., at 694. A state-court decision will also be contrary to this Court's clearly established precedent if the state court confronts a set of facts that are materially indistinguishable from a decision of this Court and nevertheless arrives at a result different from our precedent. Accordingly, in either of these two scenarios, a federal court will be unconstrained by § 2254(d)(1) because the state-court decision falls within that provision's "contrary to" clause.

On the other hand, a run-of-the-mill state-court decision applying the correct legal rule from our cases to the facts of a prisoner's case would not fit comfortably within § 2254(d)(1)'s "contrary to" clause. Assume, for example, that a state-court decision on a prisoner's ineffective-assistance claim correctly identifies *Strickland* as the controlling legal authority and, applying that framework, rejects the prisoner's claim. Quite clearly, the state-court decision would be in accord with our decision in *Strickland* as to the legal prerequisites for establishing an ineffective-assistance claim, even assuming the federal court considering the prisoner's habeas application might reach a different result applying the *Strickland* framework itself. It is difficult, however, to describe such a run-of-the-mill state-court decision as "diametrically different" from, "opposite in character or nature" from, or "mutually opposed" to *Strickland*, our clearly established precedent. Although the state-court decision may be contrary to the federal court's conception of how *Strickland* ought to be applied in that particular case, the decision is not "mutually opposed" to *Strickland* itself.

JUSTICE STEVENS would instead construe § 2254(d)(1)'s "contrary to" clause to encompass such a routine state-court decision. That construction, however, saps the "unreasonable application" clause of any meaning. If a federal habeas court can, under the "contrary to" clause, issue the writ whenever it concludes that the state court's application of clearly established federal law was incorrect, the "unreasonable application" clause becomes a nullity. We must, however, if possible, give meaning to every clause of the statute. JUSTICE STEVENS not only makes no attempt to do so, but also construes the "contrary to" clause in a manner that ensures that the "unreasonable application" clause will have no independent meaning.... We reject that expansive interpretation of the statute. Reading § 2254(d)(1)'s "contrary to" clause to permit a federal court to grant relief in cases where a state court's error is limited to the manner in which it applies Supreme Court precedent is suspect given the logical and natural fit of the neighboring "unreasonable application" clause to such cases.

The Fourth Circuit's interpretation of the "unreasonable application" clause of § 2254(d)(1) is generally correct. That court held in *Green* that a state-court decision can involve an "unreasonable application" of this Court's clearly established precedent in two ways. First, a state-court decision involves an unreasonable application of this Court's precedent if the state court identifies the correct governing legal rule from this Court's cases but unreasonably applies it to the facts of the particular state prisoner's case. Second, a state-court decision also involves an unreasonable application of this Court's precedent if the state court either unreasonably extends a legal principle from our precedent to a new context where it should not apply or unreasonably refuses to extend that principle to a new context where it should apply. See 143 F.3d, at 869–870.

A state-court decision that correctly identifies the governing legal rule but applies it unreasonably to the facts of a particular prisoner's case certainly would qualify as a decision "involv[ing] an unreasonable application of ... clearly established Federal law." Indeed, we used the almost identical phrase "application of law" to describe a state court's application of law to fact in the certiorari question we posed to the parties in [Wright v.

West, 505 U.S. 277 (1992)].[11]

The Fourth Circuit also held in *Green* that state-court decisions that unreasonably extend a legal principle from our precedent to a new context where it should not apply (or unreasonably refuse to extend a legal principle to a new context where it should apply) should be analyzed under § 2254(d)(1)'s "unreasonable application" clause. See 143 F.3d, at 869–870. Although that holding may perhaps be correct, the classification does have some problems of precision. Just as it is sometimes difficult to distinguish a mixed question of law and fact from a question of fact, it will often be difficult to identify separately those state-court decisions that involve an unreasonable application of a legal principle (or an unreasonable failure to apply a legal principle) to a new context. Indeed, on the one hand, in some cases it will be hard to distinguish a decision involving an unreasonable extension of a legal principle from a decision involving an unreasonable application of law to facts. On the other hand, in many of the same cases it will also be difficult to distinguish a decision involving an unreasonable extension of a legal principle from a decision that "arrives at a conclusion opposite to that reached by this Court on a question of law," supra, at [31]. Today's case does not require us to decide how such "extension of legal principle" cases should be treated under § 2254(d)(1). For now it is sufficient to hold that when a state-court decision unreasonably applies the law of this Court to the facts of a prisoner's case, a federal court applying § 2254(d)(1) may conclude that the state-court decision falls within that provision's "unreasonable application" clause.

B

There remains the task of defining what exactly qualifies as an "unreasonable application" of law under § 2254(d)(1). The Fourth Circuit held in *Green* that a state-court decision involves an "unreasonable application of ... clearly established Federal law" only if the state court has applied federal law "in a manner that reasonable jurists would all agree is unreasonable." 143 F.3d, at 870. The placement of this additional overlay on the "unreasonable application" clause was erroneous. . . .

Defining an "unreasonable application" by reference to a "reasonable jurist," however, is of little assistance to the courts that must apply § 2254(d)(1) and, in fact, may be misleading. Stated simply, a federal habeas court making the "unreasonable application" inquiry should ask whether the state court's application of clearly established federal law was

11. The legislative history of § 2254(d)(1) also supports this interpretation. See, e.g., 142 Cong. Rec. 7799 (1996) (remarks of Sen. Specter) ("[U]nder the bill deference will be owed to State courts' decisions on the application of Federal law to the facts. Unless it is unreasonable, a State court's decision applying the law to the facts will be upheld"); 141 Cong. Rec. 14666 (1995) (remarks of Sen. Hatch) ("[W]e allow a Federal court to overturn a State court decision only if it is contrary to clearly established Federal law or if it involves an 'unreasonable application' of clearly established Federal law to the facts").

objectively unreasonable. The federal habeas court should not transform the inquiry into a subjective one by resting its determination instead on the simple fact that at least one of the Nation's jurists has applied the relevant federal law in the same manner the state court did in the habeas petitioner's case. The "all reasonable jurists" standard would tend to mislead federal habeas courts by focusing their attention on a subjective inquiry rather than on an objective one. . . .

The term "unreasonable" is no doubt difficult to define. That said, it is a common term in the legal world and, accordingly, federal judges are familiar with its meaning. For purposes of today's opinion, the most important point is that an unreasonable application of federal law is different from an incorrect application of federal law. . . . In § 2254(d)(1), Congress specifically used the word "unreasonable," and not a term like "erroneous" or "incorrect." Under § 2254(d)(1)'s "unreasonable application" clause, then, a federal habeas court may not issue the writ simply because that court concludes in its independent judgment that the relevant state-court decision applied clearly established federal law erroneously or incorrectly. Rather, that application must also be unreasonable.

. . . . .

Throughout this discussion the meaning of the phrase "clearly established Federal law, as determined by the Supreme Court of the United States" has been put to the side. That statutory phrase refers to the holdings, as opposed to the dicta, of this Court's decisions as of the time of the relevant state-court decision. In this respect, the "clearly established Federal law" phrase bears only a slight connection to our *Teague* jurisprudence. With one caveat, whatever would qualify as an old rule under our *Teague* jurisprudence will constitute "clearly established Federal law, as determined by the Supreme Court of the United States" under § 2254(d)(1). See, e.g., Stringer v. Black, 503 U.S. 222, 228 (1992) (using term "old rule"). The one caveat, as the statutory language makes clear, is that § 2254(d)(1) restricts the source of clearly established law to this Court's jurisprudence.

In sum, § 2254(d)(1) places a new constraint on the power of a federal habeas court to grant a state prisoner's application for a writ of habeas corpus with respect to claims adjudicated on the merits in state court. Under § 2254(d)(1), the writ may issue only if one of the following two conditions is satisfied—the state-court adjudication resulted in a decision that (1) "was contrary to . . . clearly established Federal law, as determined by the Supreme Court of the United States," or (2) "involved an unreasonable application of clearly established Federal law, as determined by the Supreme Court of the United States." Under the "contrary to" clause, a federal habeas court may grant the writ if the state court arrives at a conclusion opposite to that reached by this Court on a question of law or if the state court decides a case differently than this Court has on a set of materially indistinguishable facts. Under the "unreasonable application"

91

clause, a federal habeas court may grant the writ if the state court identifies the correct governing legal principle from this Court's decisions but unreasonably applies that principle to the facts of the prisoner's case.

III

Although I disagree with JUSTICE STEVENS concerning the standard we must apply under § 2254(d)(1) in evaluating Terry Williams' claims on habeas, I agree with the Court that the Virginia Supreme Court's adjudication of Williams' claim of ineffective assistance of counsel resulted in a decision that was both contrary to and involved an unreasonable application of this Court's clearly established precedent. Specifically, I believe that the Court's discussion in Parts III and IV is correct and that it demonstrates the reasons that the Virginia Supreme Court's decision in Williams' case, even under the interpretation of § 2254(d)(1) I have set forth above, was both contrary to and involved an unreasonable application of our precedent.

First, I agree with the Court that our decision in *Strickland* undoubtedly qualifies as "clearly established Federal law, as determined by the Supreme Court of the United States," within the meaning of § 2254(d)(1).... Second, I agree that the Virginia Supreme Court's decision was contrary to that clearly established federal law to the extent it held that our decision in Lockhart v. Fretwell, 506 U.S. 364 (1993), somehow modified or supplanted the rule set forth in *Strickland*.... Specifically, the Virginia Supreme Court's decision was contrary to *Strickland* itself, where we held that a defendant demonstrates prejudice by showing "that there is a reasonable probability that, but for counsel's unprofessional errors, the result of the proceeding would have been different." 466 U.S., at 694. The Virginia Supreme Court held, in contrast, that such a focus on outcome determination was insufficient standing *alone*.... *Lockhart* does not support that broad proposition.... In his attempt to demonstrate prejudice, Williams did not rely on any "considerations that, as a matter of law, ought not inform the [prejudice] inquiry." *Lockhart*, supra, at 373 (O'CONNOR, J., concurring). Accordingly, as the Court ably explains, the Virginia Supreme Court's decision was contrary to Strickland.

. . . . .

Third, I also agree with the Court that, to the extent the Virginia Supreme Court did apply Strickland, its application was unreasonable.... As the Court correctly recounts, Williams' trial counsel failed to conduct investigation that would have uncovered substantial amounts of mitigation evidence.... The consequence of counsel's failure to conduct the requisite, diligent investigation into his client's troubling background and unique personal circumstances manifested itself during his generic, unapologetic closing argument, which provided the jury with no reasons to spare petitioner's life. More generally, the Virginia Circuit Court found that Williams' trial counsel failed to present evidence showing that Williams

92

"had a deprived and abused upbringing; that he may have been a neglected and mistreated child; that he came from an alcoholic family; ... that he was borderline mentally retarded;" and that "[his] conduct had been good in certain structured settings in his life (such as when he was incarcerated)." In addition, the Circuit Court noted the existence of "friends, neighbors and family of [Williams] who would have testified that he had redeeming qualities." Based on its consideration of all of this evidence, the same trial judge that originally found Williams' death sentence "justified and warranted," concluded that trial counsel's deficient performance prejudiced Williams, and accordingly recommended that Williams be granted a new sentencing hearing. The Virginia Supreme Court's decision reveals an obvious failure to consider the totality of the omitted mitigation evidence.... For that reason, and the remaining factors discussed in the Court's opinion, I believe that the Virginia Supreme Court's decision "involved an unreasonable application of ... clearly established Federal law, as determined by the Supreme Court of the United States."

Accordingly, although I disagree with the interpretation of § 2254(d)(1) set forth in Part II of JUSTICE STEVENS' opinion, I join Parts I, III, and IV of the Court's opinion and concur in the judgment of reversal.

■ CHIEF JUSTICE REHNQUIST, with whom JUSTICE SCALIA and JUSTICE THOMAS join, concurring in part and dissenting in part.

I agree with the Court's interpretation of 28 U.S.C. § 2254(d)(1), but disagree with its decision to grant habeas relief in this case.[12]

[12. Chen, Shadow Law: Reasonable Unreasonableness, Habeas Theory, and the Nature of Legal Rules, 2 Buff.Crim.L.Rev. 535 (1999), provides an excellent overview of the meaning and effect of new § 2254(d)(1). It was written before the Supreme Court resolved these issues in Williams v. Taylor.

The Supreme Court decided two AEDPA cases styled "Williams v. Taylor" on the same day, April 18, 2000. In the principal case, involving construction of new § 2254(d)(1), the petitioner was Terry Williams. In the other case, Williams v. Taylor, 529 U.S. 420 (2000), the petitioner was Michael Wayne Williams. In this latter case the Court construed new § 2254(e)(2), which prohibits a federal district court from holding an evidentiary hearing with respect to a claim as to which the habeas applicant "has failed to develop the factual basis ... in State court proceedings." A unanimous Court held that this imposes a "due diligence" rather than a "no-fault" standard. Under this standard the applicant's failure to develop in state court a factual basis for his juror bias and prosecutorial misconduct claims was excused upon a showing that the allegedly biased juror had lied during voir dire, with the knowledge and tacit acquiescence of the prosecutor.

In Slack v. McDaniel, 529 U.S. 473 (2000), the Court adopted a lenient rule for issuance of the certificate of appealability required by AEDPA's § 2253(c), and (here applying pre-AEDPA law) also held that a habeas petition which was filed after an initial petition had been dismissed on nonexhaustion grounds was not barred as a "second or successive petition" under Rule 9(b) of the Rules Governing Section 2254 Cases in the Federal District Courts.

Bell v. Cone, 535 U.S. ___, 122 S.Ct. 1843 (2002), makes clear that the principal case of Terry Williams v. Taylor left plenty of teeth in 28 U.S.C. § 2254(d)(1). As amended by AEDPA, this provision bars federal habeas review of the merits of a state court decision that may be wrong as a matter of

93

federal law, but is not *so* wrong that it can be said either to be "contrary to," or to "involve[] an unreasonable application of, clearly established Federal law, as determined by the Supreme Court of the United States." Eight members of the Court joined Chief Justice Rehnquist's opinion reversing the granting of habeas relief by the Sixth Circuit on Sixth Amendment ineffective-assistance-of-counsel (IAC) grounds in a capital case in which defense counsel presented no mitigating evidence at the penalty phase, and waived final argument. The state court had upheld Cone's death sentence, choosing to apply the IAC standard of Strickland v. Washington, 466 U.S. 668 (1984)(establishing a strong presumption against IAC when counsel is present and appears to exercise professional judgment, however poorly conducted the defense may appear in hindsight), rather than that of its companion case, United States v. Cronic, 466 U.S. 648 (1984) (presuming IAC when there is such a complete adversarial breakdown that actually or essentially no counsel was present to represent the defendant). The Supreme Court decided that the state court had not acted "contrary to ... clearly established Federal law" by applying the wrong precedent, i.e., the pro-prosecution rule of Strickland rather than the pro-defendant rule of Cronic. "Here, respondent's argument is not that his counsel failed to oppose the prosecution throughout the sentencing proceeding, as a whole, but that his counsel failed to do so at specific points. For purposes of distinguishing between the rule of *Strickland* and that of *Cronic*, this difference is not of degree but of kind." 535 U.S. at ___, 122 S.Ct. at 1851. This left as Cone's last hope his alternative argument that § 2254(d)(1) permitted the granting of habeas relief because the state court "applied *Strickland*

to the facts of his case in an objectively unreasonable manner." 535 U.S. at ___, 122 S.Ct. at 1852. Without endorsing the state court's application of Strickland, the majority concluded that "we cannot say that the state court's application of Strickland's attorney-performance standard was objectively unreasonable." 535 U.S. at ___, 122 S.Ct. at 1854.

What makes this a compelling application of the restrictive standards of post-AEDPA § 2254(d)(1) are the additional facts disclosed in the dissenting opinion of Justice Stevens: "respondent's counsel was, subsequent to trial, diagnosed with a mental illness that rendered him unqualified to practice law, and that apparently led to his suicide." 535 U.S. at ___, 122 S.Ct. at 1854 (dissenting opn.). Justice Stevens stood alone in concluding that this twist justified the Sixth Circuit's determination that this was a case governed by Cronic, not Strickland, and thus that the state court had applied Strickland "contrary to" the clearly established precedent of Cronic. For another recent IAC case discussing the Strickland–Cronic boundary purely as a matter of Sixth Amendment law, free of jurisdictional or issue-preclusion complications, see Mickens v. Taylor, 535 U.S. ___, 122 S.Ct. 1237 (2002). Mickens held, 5–4, that absent a specific showing that the conflict adversely affected counsel's representation of a defendant convicted of capital murder, the fact that defendant's appointed counsel was also serving as appointed counsel for the murder victim at the time of his death (and that both appointments had been made by the same judge of the state juvenile court) did not constitute IAC and hence furnished no ground for federal habeas relief.

Page 527. Add to Footnote 100

After granting certiorari and hearing oral argument in Fiore v. White, the Supreme Court decided unanimously to certify to the Supreme Court of Pennsylvania the question whether an earlier decision of that state court—interpreting a state statute in a codefendant's case in a way that

meant that as a matter of law petitioner Fiore was innocent of the crime for which he was convicted—established new law in Pennsylvania or merely resolved controversy about the meaning of the law as it existed at the time of Fiore's conviction. 528 U.S. 23 (1999). The Supreme Court of

Pennsylvania duly certified that its decision had simply settled the question of what Pennsylvania law had required all along as an element of the crime for which Fiore had been convicted—even though the Supreme Court of Pennsylvania had seen fit to deny Fiore any postconviction relief after its decision in the codefendant's case had made clear that Fiore had been wrongfully convicted because on the undisputed facts of his case he had not committed all the elements of the relevant crime. The United States Supreme Court again acted unanimously in holding that in these circumstances, where he was not relying on some "new rule" of state law but simply on the authoritatively construed law under which he was convicted, Fiore had a due process right to federal habeas relief from his conviction of a crime of which he was actually innocent. Fiore v. White, 531 U.S. 225 (2001) (per curiam).

In Horn v. Banks, 536 U.S. ___, 122 S.Ct. 2147 (2002) (per curiam), the Court emphatically made clear that the nonretroactivity of an arguably new rule of constitutional law under Teague v. Lane, 489 U.S. 288 (1989), remains a distinct inquiry that if asserted in federal court must be resolved before determining whether a state court's application of the rule was "contrary to, or involved an unreasonable application of" the clearly established precedent of the Supreme Court and hence properly the basis for federal habeas relief under 28 U.S.C. § 2254(d)(1) as amended by AEDPA. Under Caspari v. Bohlen, 510 U.S. 383 (1994), Teague analysis is not required only if the state fails to argue in federal court that Teague forecloses federal habeas relief. In Horn the Court declared that AEDPA did not alter the course of analysis under Teague and Caspari. Even if the state courts deny post-conviction relief on the merits, and even if this is contrary to the clearly established precedent of the Supreme Court articulating the arguably new rule relied upon by the petitioner, federal habeas relief is barred if the state asserts Teague in federal court unless the federal court first finds that Teague does not bar retroactive application of the rule in question.

The Court's two major capital-punishment decisions at the end of the 2001 Term provide useful illustrations of Teague's two exceptions to its general ban on giving retrospective effect to new rules of constitutional law. (These exceptions are discussed in the first paragraph of footnote 100 as printed at pages 527–529 of the main volume.)The first of these cases, Atkins v. Virginia, 536 U.S. ___, ___, 122 S.Ct. 2242, 2252 (2002), declared expressly that "the Constitution 'places a substantive restriction on the State's power to take the life' of a mentally retarded offender." By thus resolving that the new rule announced in Atkins was substantive rather than procedural in nature, the Court all but guaranteed the retrospectivity of that rule under the first of the Teague exceptions. The second case, Ring v. Arizona, 536 U.S. ___, 122 S.Ct. 2428 (2002), declared that "[t]he right to trial by jury guaranteed by the Sixth Amendment would be senselessly diminished [unless] it encompassed . . . the factfinding necessary to put [a defendant] to death," and thus held that a defendant who had requested jury trial was entitled to have a jury, not a judge, determine the existence of the aggravating factors required for a capital sentence. While possible, it seems unlikely that the Court will later determine that this procedural requirement as to how aggravating factors are to be adjudicated is such a bedrock rule of procedural fairness as to be part of the "ordered liberty" that requires "watershed" new rules of constitutional criminal procedure to be given retrospective effect under the second of the Teague exceptions. It is noteworthy in this connection that Ring was an extension of the scope of the Sixth Amendment's right to jury trial as established in Apprendi v. New Jersey, 530 U.S. 466 (2000), requiring jury determination of aggravating factors used to increase the term of a non-capital sentence beyond the statutory maximum authorized for the crime of which the defendant had been convicted by a jury. To date all six circuits that have ruled on the issue have found that Teague bars retrospective application of Apprendi's new rule on the scope of the Sixth Amendment's right to jury trial. See Curtis v. United States, ___ F.3d ___, ___, 2002 WL 1332817 (7th Cir.2002) (collecting cases).

95

Page 529. Insert at the end of Section 9 of Chapter VIII, immediately before the beginning of Section 10.

Lee v. Kemna

Supreme Court of the United States, 2002.
534 U.S. 362, 122 S.Ct. 877, 151 L.Ed.2d 820.

■ JUSTICE GINSBURG delivered the opinion of the Court.

Petitioner Remon Lee asserts that a Missouri trial court deprived him of due process when the court refused to grant an overnight continuance of his trial. Lee sought the continuance to locate subpoenaed, previously present, but suddenly missing witnesses key to his defense against felony charges. On direct review, the Missouri Court of Appeals disposed of the case on a state procedural ground. That court found the continuance motion defective under the State's rules. It therefore declined to consider the merits of Lee's plea that the trial court had denied him a fair opportunity to present a defense. Whether the state ground dispositive in the Missouri Court of Appeals is adequate to preclude federal habeas corpus review is the question we here consider and decide.

On the third day of his trial, Lee was convicted of first-degree murder and armed criminal action. His sole affirmative defense was an alibi; Lee maintained he was in California, staying with his family, when the Kansas City crimes for which he was indicted occurred. Lee's mother, stepfather, and sister voluntarily came to Missouri to testify on his behalf. They were sequestered in the courthouse at the start of the trial's third day. For reasons then unknown, they were not in the courthouse later in the day when defense counsel sought to present their testimony. Discovering their absence, defense counsel moved for a continuance until the next morning so that he could endeavor to locate the three witnesses and bring them back to court.

The trial judge denied the motion, stating that it looked to him as though the witnesses had "in effect abandoned the defendant" and that, for personal reasons, he would "not be able to be [in court the next day] to try the case." Furthermore, he had "another case set for trial" the next weekday. The trial resumed without pause, no alibi witnesses testified, and the jury found Lee guilty as charged.

Neither the trial judge nor the prosecutor identified any procedural flaw in the presentation or content of Lee's motion for a continuance. The Missouri Court of Appeals, however, held the denial of the motion proper because Lee's counsel had failed to comply with Missouri Supreme Court Rules not relied upon or even mentioned in the trial court: Rule 24.09, which requires that continuance motions be in written form, accompanied by an affidavit; and Rule 24.10, which sets out the showings a movant must make to gain a continuance grounded on the absence of witnesses.

We hold that the Missouri Rules, as injected into this case by the state appellate court, did not constitute a state ground adequate to bar federal habeas review. Caught in the midst of a murder trial and unalerted to any procedural defect in his presentation, defense counsel could hardly be expected to divert his attention from the proceedings rapidly unfolding in the courtroom and train, instead, on preparation of a written motion and affidavit. Furthermore, the trial court, at the time Lee moved for a continuance, had in clear view the information needed to rule intelligently on the merits of the motion. Beyond doubt, Rule 24.10 serves the State's important interest in regulating motions for a continuance—motions readily susceptible to use as a delaying tactic. But under the circumstances of this case, we hold that petitioner Lee, having substantially, if imperfectly, made the basic showings Rule 24.10 prescribes, qualifies for adjudication of his federal, due process claim. His asserted right to defend should not depend on a formal "ritual ... [that] would further no perceivable state interest." Osborne v. Ohio, 495 U.S. 103, 124 (1990) (quoting James v. Kentucky, 466 U.S. 341, 349 (1984) (in turn quoting Staub v. City of Baxley, 355 U.S. 313, 320 (1958))) (internal quotation marks omitted).

I

On August 27, 1992, Reginald Rhodes shot and killed Steven Shelby on a public street in Kansas City, Missouri. He then jumped into the passenger side of a waiting truck, which sped away. Rhodes pleaded guilty, and Remon Lee, the alleged getaway driver, was tried for first-degree murder and armed criminal action.

Lee's trial took place within the span of three days in February 1994. His planned alibi defense—that he was in California with his family at the time of the murder—surfaced at each stage of the proceedings....

The planned alibi defense figured prominently in counsels' opening statements on day two of Lee's trial. The prosecutor, at the close of her statement, said she expected an alibi defense from Lee and would present testimony to disprove it. Defense counsel, in his opening statement, described the alibi defense in detail, telling the jury that the evidence would show Lee was not in Kansas City, and therefore could not have engaged in crime there, in August 1992. Specifically, defense counsel said three close family members would testify that Lee came to visit them in Ventura, California, in July 1992 and stayed through the end of October. Lee's mother and stepfather would say they picked him up from the airport at the start of his visit and returned him there at the end. Lee's sister would testify that Lee resided with her and her four children during this time. All three would affirm that they saw Lee regularly throughout his unbroken sojourn.

During the prosecution case, two eyewitnesses to the shooting identified Lee as the driver. The first, Reginald Williams, admitted during cross-examination that he had told Lee's first defense counsel in a taped interview that Rhodes, not Lee, was the driver.... The second eyewitness,

97

William Sanders, was unable to pick Lee out of a photographic array on the day of the shooting. . . .

Two other witnesses, Rhonda Shelby and Lynne Bryant, were called by the prosecutor. Each testified that she knew Lee and had seen him in Kansas City the night before the murder. Both said Lee was with Rhodes, who had asked where Steven Shelby (the murder victim) was. . . . The State offered no physical evidence connecting Lee to the murder and did not suggest a motive.

The defense case began at 10:25 a.m. on the third and final day of trial. Two impeachment witnesses testified that morning. Just after noon, counsel met with the trial judge in chambers for a charge conference. At that meeting, the judge apparently agreed to give an alibi instruction submitted by Lee.[34]

At some point in the late morning or early afternoon, the alibi witnesses left the courthouse. Just after one o'clock, Lee took the stand outside the presence of the jury and, for the record, responded to his counsel's questions concerning his knowledge of the witnesses' unanticipated absence. Lee, under oath, stated that Gladys and James Edwards and Laura Lee had voluntarily traveled from California to testify on his behalf. He affirmed his counsel's representations that the three witnesses, then staying with Lee's uncle in Kansas City, had met with Lee's counsel and received subpoenas from him; he similarly affirmed that the witnesses had met with a Kansas City police officer, who interviewed them on behalf of the prosecutor. Lee said he had seen his sister, mother, and stepfather in the courthouse that morning at 8:30 and later during a recess.

On discovering the witnesses' absence, Lee could not call them at his uncle's house because there was no phone on the premises. He asked his girlfriend to try to find the witnesses, but she was unable to do so. Although Lee did not know the witnesses' whereabouts at that moment, he said he knew "in fact they didn't go back to California" because "they had some ministering . . . to do" in Kansas City both Thursday and Friday evenings. He asked for "a couple hours' continuance [to] try to locate them, because it's very valuable to my case." Defense counsel subsequently moved for a continuance until the next morning, to gain time to enforce the subpoenas he had served on the witnesses. The trial judge responded that he could not hold court the next day because "my daughter is going to be in the hospital all day . . . [s]o I've got to stay with her."

After a brief further exchange between court and counsel, the judge denied the continuance request. . . .

. . . . .

34. That Lee had submitted an alibi instruction during the charge conference became apparent when the trial judge, delivering the charge, began to read the proposed instruction. He was interrupted by the prosecutor and defense counsel, who reminded him that the instruction was no longer necessary.

When the jurors returned, defense counsel informed them that the three witnesses from California he had planned to call "were here and have gone"; further, counsel did not "know why they've gone." The defense then rested....

After deliberating for three hours, the jury convicted Lee on both counts. He was subsequently sentenced to prison for life without possibility of parole.

. . . . .

The Missouri Court of Appeals affirmed Lee's conviction and the denial of postconviction relief. State v. Lee, 935 S.W.2d 689 (1996). The appellate court first noted that Lee's continuance motion was oral and therefore did not comply with Missouri Supreme Court Rule 24.09 (Rule 24.09), which provides that such applications shall be in written form, accompanied by an affidavit. "Thus," the Court of Appeals said, "the trial court could have properly denied the motion for a failure to comply with Rule 24.09." Even assuming the adequacy of Lee's oral motion, the court continued, the application "was made without the factual showing required by Rule 24.10." The court did not say which components of Rule 24.10 were unsatisfied. "When a denial to grant a motion for continuance is based on a deficient application," the Court of Appeals next said, "it does not constitute an abuse of discretion." Lee's subsequent motions for rehearing and transfer to the Missouri Supreme Court were denied.

In January 1998, Lee, proceeding pro se, filed an application for writ of habeas corpus in the United States District Court for the Western District of Missouri. Lee once again challenged the denial of his continuance motion. He appended affidavits from the three witnesses, each of whom swore to Lee's alibi; sister, mother, and stepfather alike stated that they had left the courthouse while the trial was underway because a court officer told them their testimony would not be needed that day. Lee maintained that the State had engineered the witnesses' departure; accordingly, he asserted that prosecutorial misconduct, not anything over which he had control, prompted the need for a continuance.

The District Court denied the writ. The witnesses' affidavits were not cognizable in federal habeas proceedings, the court held, because Lee could have offered them to the state courts but failed to do so. The Federal District Court went on to reject Lee's continuance claim, finding in the Missouri Court of Appeals' invocation of Rule 24.10 an adequate and independent state-law ground barring further review.

The Court of Appeals for the Eighth Circuit granted a certificate of appealability, limited to the question whether Lee's "due process rights were violated by the state trial court's failure to allow him a continuance," and affirmed the denial of Lee's habeas petition. 213 F.3d 1037 (2000) (per curiam).... "The Missouri Court of Appeals rejected Lee's claim because his motion for a continuance did not comply with [Rules] 24.09 and 24.10," the Eighth Circuit . . . stated. Thus, that court concluded, "the claim was procedurally defaulted." 213 F.3d, at 1038.

. . . . .

We granted Lee's pro se petition for a writ of certiorari, 531 U.S. 1189 (2001), and appointed counsel, 532 U.S. 956 (2001). We now vacate the Court of Appeals judgment.

II

This Court will not take up a question of federal law presented in a case "if the decision of [the state] court rests on a state law ground that is *independent* of the federal question and *adequate* to support the judgment." Coleman v. Thompson, 501 U.S. 722, 729 (1991) (emphases added). The rule applies with equal force whether the state-law ground is substantive or procedural. We first developed the independent and adequate state ground doctrine in cases on direct review from state courts, and later applied it as well "in deciding whether federal district courts should address the claims of state prisoners in habeas corpus actions." Ibid. "[T]he adequacy of state procedural bars to the assertion of federal questions," we have recognized, is not within the State's prerogative finally to decide; rather, adequacy "is itself a federal question." Douglas v. Alabama, 380 U.S. 415, 422 (1965).

Lee does not suggest that Rules 24.09 and 24.10, as brought to bear on this case by the Missouri Court of Appeals, depended in any way on federal law. Nor does he question the general applicability of the two codified Rules. He does maintain that both Rules—addressed initially to Missouri trial courts, but in his case invoked only at the appellate stage—are inadequate, under the extraordinary circumstances of this case, to close out his federal, fair-opportunity-to-defend claim. We now turn to that dispositive issue.

Ordinarily, violation of "firmly established and regularly followed" state rules—for example, those involved in this case—will be adequate to foreclose review of a federal claim. James v. Kentucky, 466 U.S. 341, 348 (1984); see Ford v. Georgia, 498 U.S. 411, 422–424 (1991). There are, however, exceptional cases in which exorbitant application of a generally sound rule renders the state ground inadequate to stop consideration of a federal question. See Davis v. Wechsler, 263 U.S. 22, 24 (1923) (Holmes, J.) ("Whatever springes the State may set for those who are endeavoring to assert rights that the State confers, the assertion of federal rights, when plainly and reasonably made, is not to be defeated under the name of local practice."). This case fits within that limited category.

Our analysis and conclusion are informed and controlled by Osborne v. Ohio, 495 U.S. 103 (1990). There, the Court considered Osborne's objections that his child pornography conviction violated due process because the trial judge had not required the government to prove two elements of the alleged crime: lewd exhibition and scienter. Id., at 107, 122–125. The

Ohio Supreme Court held the constitutional objections procedurally barred because Osborne had failed to object contemporaneously to the judge's charge, which did not instruct the jury that it could convict only for conduct that satisfied both the scienter and the lewdness elements. . . .

We agreed with the State that Osborne's failure to urge the trial court to instruct the jury on scienter qualified as an "adequate state-law ground [to] preven[t] us from reaching Osborne's due process contention on that point." 495 U.S., at 123. Ohio law, which was not in doubt, required proof of scienter unless the applicable statute specified otherwise. The State's contemporaneous objection rule, we observed, "serves the State's important interest in ensuring that counsel do their part in preventing trial courts from providing juries with erroneous instructions." Id., at 123.

"With respect to the trial court's failure to instruct on lewdness, however, we reach[ed] a different conclusion." Ibid. Counsel for Osborne had made his position on that essential element clear in a motion to dismiss overruled just before trial, and the trial judge, "in no uncertain terms," id., at 124, had rejected counsel's argument. After a brief trial, the judge charged the jury in line with his ruling against Osborne on the pretrial motion to dismiss. Counsel's failure to object to the charge by reasserting the argument he had made unsuccessfully on the motion to dismiss, we held, did not deter our disposition of the constitutional question. "Given this sequence of events," we explained, it was proper to "reach Osborne's [second] due process claim," for Osborne's attorney had "pressed the issue of the State's failure of proof on lewdness before the trial court and . . . nothing would be gained by requiring Osborne's lawyer to object a second time, specifically to the jury instructions." Ibid. In other words, although we did not doubt the general applicability of the Ohio Rule of Criminal Procedure requiring contemporaneous objection to jury charges, we nevertheless concluded that, in this atypical instance, the Rule would serve "no perceivable state interest." Ibid. (internal quotation marks omitted).

Our decision, we added in *Osborne*, followed from "the general principle that an objection which is ample and timely to bring the alleged federal error to the attention of the trial court and enable it to take appropriate corrective action is sufficient to serve legitimate state interests, and therefore sufficient to preserve the claim for review here." Id., at 125 (quoting *Douglas*, 380 U.S., at 422 (internal quotation marks omitted)). This general principle, and the unusual "sequence of events" before us—rapidly unfolding events that Lee and his counsel could not have foreseen, and for which they were not at all responsible—similarly guide our judgment in this case.

The dissent strives mightily to distinguish *Osborne*, an opinion Justices Kennedy and Scalia joined, but cannot do so convincingly. . . .

. . . . .

Three considerations, in combination, lead us to conclude that this case falls within the small category of cases in which asserted state grounds are

101

inadequate to block adjudication of a federal claim. First, when the trial judge denied Lee's motion, he stated a reason that could not have been countered by a perfect motion for continuance. The judge said he could not carry the trial over until the next day because he had to be with his daughter in the hospital; the judge further informed counsel that another scheduled trial prevented him from concluding Lee's case on the following business day. Although the judge hypothesized that the witnesses had "abandoned" Lee, he had not "a scintilla of evidence or a shred of information" on which to base this supposition, 213 F.3d, at 1040 (Bennett, C. J., dissenting).

Second, no published Missouri decision directs flawless compliance with Rules 24.09 and 24.10 in the unique circumstances this case presents—the sudden, unanticipated, and at the time unexplained disappearance of critical, subpoenaed witnesses on what became the trial's last day. Lee's predicament, from all that appears, was one Missouri courts had not confronted before. "[A]lthough [the rules themselves] may not [have been] novel, ... [their] application to the facts here was." Sullivan v. Little Hunting Park, Inc., 396 U.S. 229, 245 (1969) (Harlan, J., dissenting).

Third and most important ... Lee substantially complied with Missouri's key Rule. . . . In sum, we are drawn to the conclusion reached by the Eighth Circuit dissenter: "[A]ny seasoned trial lawyer would agree" that insistence on a written continuance application, supported by an affidavit, "in the midst of trial upon the discovery that subpoenaed witnesses are suddenly absent, would be so bizarre as to inject an Alice-in-Wonderland quality into the proceedings." 213 F.3d, at 1047.

· · · · ·

Rule 24.10, like other state and federal rules of its genre, serves a governmental interest of undoubted legitimacy. It is designed to arm trial judges with the information needed to rule reliably on a motion to delay a scheduled criminal trial. The Rule's essential requirements, however, were substantially met in this case. Few transcript pages need be read to reveal the information called for by Rule 24.10. "[N]othing would [have] be[en] gained by requiring" Lee's counsel to recapitulate in (a), (b), (c), (d) order the showings the Rule requires. . . . "Where it is inescapable that the defendant sought to invoke the substance of his federal right, the asserted state-law defect in form must be more evident than it is here." James v. Kentucky, 466 U.S., at 351.[35]

The dissent critiques at great length Henry v. Mississippi, 379 U.S. 443

---

35. The dissent, indulging in hyperbole, describes our narrow opinion as a "comb" and "searc[h]" order to lower courts. We hold, simply and only, that *Lee* satisfied Rule 24.10's essential elements. [W]e place no burden *on courts* to rummage through a ponderous trial transcript in search of an excuse for a defense counsel's lapse. The dissent, in this and much else, tilts at a windmill of its own invention.

(1965), a case on which we do not rely in reaching our decision.[36] This protracted exercise is a prime example of the dissent's vigorous attack on an imaginary opinion that bears scant, if any, resemblance to the actual decision rendered today. We chart no new course. We merely apply *Osborne's* sound reasoning and limited holding to the circumstances of this case. If the dissent's shrill prediction that today's decision will disrupt our federal system were accurate, we would have seen clear signals of such disruption in the eleven years since *Osborne*. The absence of even dim distress signals demonstrates both the tight contours of *Osborne* and the groundlessness of the dissent's frantic forecast of doom. See United States v. Travers, 514 F.2d 1171, 1174 (CA2 1974) (Friendly, J.) ("Cassandra-like predictions in dissent are not a sure guide to the breadth of the majority's ruling").

. . . . .

To summarize, there was in this case no reference whatever in the trial court to Rules 24.09 and 24.10, the purported procedural impediments the Missouri Court of Appeals later pressed. Nor is there any indication that formally perfect compliance with the Rules would have changed the trial court's decision. Furthermore, no published Missouri decision demands unmodified application of the Rules in the urgent situation Lee's case presented. Finally, the purpose of the Rules was served by Lee's submissions both immediately before and at the short trial. Under the special circumstances so combined, we conclude that no adequate state-law ground hinders consideration of Lee's federal claim.[37]

Because both the District Court and the Court of Appeals held Lee's due process claim procedurally barred, neither court addressed it on the merits. We remand the case for that purpose. See National Collegiate

---

36. *Henry* has been called "radical," ... R. Fallon, D. Meltzer, & D. Shapiro, Hart and Wechsler's The Federal Courts and the Federal System 584 (4th ed.1996) ..., not for pursuing an "as applied" approach, as the dissent states, but for suggesting that the failure to comply with an anterior procedure was cured by compliance with some subsequent procedure. See id., at 584–585. In *Henry*, the Court indicated that although there was no contemporaneous objection at trial to the admission of evidence alleged to have been derived from an unconstitutional search, a directed verdict motion made at the end of the prosecution's case was an adequate substitute. 379 U.S., at 448–449. Nothing of the sort is involved in this case. Lee is not endeavoring to designate some later motion, e.g., one for a new trial, as an adequate substitute for a continuance motion. The question here is whether the movant must enunciate again, when making the right motion at the right time, supporting statements plainly and repeatedly made the days before....

37. In view of this disposition, we do not reach further questions raised by Lee, i.e., whether he has shown "cause" and "prejudice" to excuse any default, Wainwright v. Sykes, 433 U.S. 72, 90–91 (1977), or has made sufficient showing of "actual innocence" under Schlup v. Delo, 513 U.S. 298, 315 (1995), to warrant a hearing of the kind ordered in that case.

103

Athletic Assn. v. Smith, 525 U.S. 459, 470 (1999) (We ordinarily "do not decide in the first instance issues not decided below.").

* * *

For the reasons stated, the judgment of the United States Court of Appeals for the Eighth Circuit is vacated, and the case is remanded for further proceedings consistent with this opinion.

It is so ordered.

■ JUSTICE KENNEDY, with whom JUSTICE SCALIA and JUSTICE THOMAS join, dissenting.

The Court's decision commits us to a new and, in my view, unwise course. Its contextual approach places unnecessary and unwarranted new responsibilities on state trial judges, injects troubling instability into the criminal justice system, and reaches the wrong result even under its own premises. These considerations prompt my respectful dissent.

I

The rule that an adequate state procedural ground can bar federal review of a constitutional claim has always been "about federalism," Coleman v. Thompson, 501 U.S. 722, 726 (1991), for it respects state rules of procedure while ensuring that they do not discriminate against federal rights. The doctrine originated in cases on direct review, where the existence of an independent and adequate state ground deprives this Court of jurisdiction. The rule applies with equal force, albeit for somewhat different reasons, when federal courts review the claims of state prisoners in habeas corpus proceedings, where ignoring procedural defaults would circumvent the jurisdictional limits of direct review and "undermine the State's interest in enforcing its laws." Id., at 731.

Given these considerations of comity and federalism, a procedural ground will be deemed inadequate only when the state rule "force[s] resort to an arid ritual of meaningless form." Staub v. City of Baxley, 355 U.S. 313, 320 (1958). *Staub*'s formulation was imprecise, but the cases that followed clarified the two essential components of the adequate state ground inquiry: first, the defendant must have notice of the rule; and second, the State must have a legitimate interest in its enforcement.

The Court need not determine whether the requirement of Missouri Supreme Court Rule 24.09 that all continuance motions be made in writing would withstand scrutiny under the second part of this test.... Even if it could be assumed, for the sake of argument, that Rule 24.09 would not afford defendants a fair opportunity to raise a federal claim, the same cannot be said of Rule 24.10. The latter Rule simply requires a party requesting a continuance on account of missing witnesses to explain why it is needed, and the Rule serves an undoubted and important state interest in facilitating the orderly management of trials. Other States have similar requirements.... The Court's explicit depreciation of Rule 24.10—and implicit depreciation of its many counterparts—is inconsistent with the respect due to state courts and state proceedings.

A

The initial step of the adequacy inquiry considers whether the State has put litigants on notice of the rule. The Court will disregard state procedures not firmly established and regularly followed....

. . . . .

Lee was on notice of the applicability of Rule 24.10, and the Court appears to recognize as much. The consideration most important to the Court's analysis ... relates not to this initial question, but rather to the second part of the adequacy inquiry, which asks whether the rule serves a legitimate state interest. Here, too, in my respectful view, the Court errs.

B

A defendant's failure to comply with a firmly established and regularly followed rule has been deemed an inadequate state ground only when the State had no legitimate interest in the rule's enforcement.... Most state procedures are supported by various legitimate interests, so established rules have been set aside only when they appeared to be calculated to discriminate against federal law, or, as one treatise puts it, they did not afford the defendant "a reasonable opportunity to assert federal rights." 16B Charles Alan Wright, Arthur R. Miller, & Edward H. Cooper, Federal Practice and Procedure, § 4027, p. 392 (2d ed.1996)....

In light of this standard, the adequacy of Rule 24.10 has been demonstrated. Delays in criminal trials can be "a distinct reproach to the administration of justice," Powell v. Alabama, 287 U.S. 45, 59 (1932), and States have a strong interest in ensuring that continuances are granted only when necessary. Rule 24.10 anticipates that at certain points during a trial, important witnesses may not be available. In these circumstances, a continuance may be appropriate if the movant makes certain required representations demonstrating good cause to believe the continuance would make a real difference to the case.

Yet the Court deems Lee's default inadequate because, it says, to the extent feasible under the circumstances, he substantially complied with the Rule's essential requirements. These precise terms have not been used in the Court's adequacy jurisprudence before, and it is necessary to explore their implications. The argument is not that Missouri has no interest in enforcing compliance with the Rule in general, but rather that it had no interest in enforcing full compliance in this particular case. This is so, the Court holds, because the Rule's essential purposes were substantially served by other procedural devices, such as opening statement, voir dire, and Lee's testimony on the stand.... So viewed, the Court's substantial-

105

compliance terminology begins to look more familiar: It simply paraphrases the flawed analytical approach first proposed by the Court in Henry v. Mississippi, 379 U.S. 443 (1965), but not further ratified or in fact used to set aside a procedural rule until today.

Before *Henry,* the adequacy inquiry focused on the general legitimacy of the established procedural rule, overlooking its violation only when the rule itself served no legitimate interest.... *Henry* was troubling, and much criticized, because it injected an as-applied factor into the equation.... The petitioner in *Henry* had defaulted his Fourth Amendment claim in state court by failing to lodge a contemporaneous objection to the admission of the contested evidence. Despite conceding the legitimate state interest in enforcing this common rule, the Court vacated the state-court judgment, proposing that the default may have been inadequate because the rule's "purpose ... may have been substantially served by petitioner's motion at the close of the State's evidence asking for a directed verdict." Henry v. Mississippi, supra, at 448. The suggestion, then, was that a violation of a rule serving a legitimate state interest may be ignored when, in the peculiar circumstances of a given case, the defendant utilized some other procedure serving the same interest.

For all *Henry* possessed in mischievous potential, however, it lacked significant precedential effect. *Henry* itself did not hold the asserted state ground inadequate; instead it remanded for the state court to determine whether "petitioner's counsel deliberately bypassed the opportunity to make timely objection in the state court." 379 U.S., at 449–453. The cornerstone of that analysis, the deliberate-bypass standard of Fay v. Noia, 372 U.S. 391, 426–434 (1963), later was limited to its facts in Wainwright v. Sykes, 433 U.S. 72, 87–88 (1977), and then put to rest in Coleman v. Thompson, 501 U.S., at 750. Subsequent cases maintained the pre-*Henry* focus on the general validity of the challenged state practice, either declining to cite *Henry* or framing its holding in innocuous terms....

There is no meaningful distinction between the *Henry* Court's analysis and the standard the Court applies today, and this surprising reinvigoration of the case-by-case approach is contrary to the principles of federalism underlying our habeas corpus jurisprudence. Procedural rules, like the substantive laws they implement, are the products of sovereignty and democratic processes. The States have weighty interests in enforcing rules that protect the integrity and uniformity of trials, even when "the reason for the rule does not clearly apply." Staub v. City of Baxley, 355 U.S., at 333 (Frankfurter, J., dissenting). Regardless of the particular facts in extraordinary cases, then, Missouri has a freestanding interest in Rule 24.10 as a rule.

By ignoring that interest, the majority's approach invites much mischief at criminal trials, and the burden imposed upon States and their courts will be heavy. All requirements of a rule are, in the rulemaker's view, essential to fulfill its purposes; imperfect compliance is thus, by definition, not compliance at all. Yet the State's sound judgment on these matters can now be overridden by a federal court, which may determine for itself, given its own understanding of the rule's purposes, whether a requirement was essential or compliance was substantial in the unique circumstances of any given case. Henceforth, each time a litigant does not comply with an established state procedure, the judge must inquire, even "in the midst of trial, . . . whether noncompliance should be excused because some alternative procedure might be deemed adequate in the particular situation." [R. Fallon, D. Meltzer, & D. Shapiro, Hart and Wechsler's The Federal Courts and the Federal System] 585 [(4th ed.1996)]. The trial courts, then the state appellate courts, and, in the end, the federal habeas courts in numerous instances must comb through the full transcript and trial record, searching for ways in which the defendant might have substantially complied with the essential requirements of an otherwise broken rule.

The Court seeks to ground its renewal of *Henry's* long-quiescent dictum in our more recent decision in Osborne v. Ohio, 495 U.S., at 122–125. Though isolated statements in *Osborne* might appear to support the majority's approach—or, for that matter, *Henry's* approach—*Osborne's* holding does not.

. . . . .

In sum, Rule 24.10 served legitimate state interests, both as a general matter and as applied to the facts of this case. Lee's failure to comply was an adequate state ground, and the Court's contrary determination does not bode well for the adequacy doctrine or federalism.

II

A federal court could consider the merits of Lee's defaulted federal claim if he had shown cause for the default and prejudice therefrom, see Wainwright v. Sykes, 433 U.S., at 90–91, or made out a compelling case of actual innocence, see Schlup v. Delo, 513 U.S. 298, 314–315 (1995). He has done neither.

As to the first question, Lee says the sudden disappearance of his witnesses caused him to neglect Rule 24.10. In one sense, of course, he is right, for he would not have requested the continuance, much less failed to comply with Rule 24.10, if his witnesses had not left the courthouse. The argument, though, is unavailing. The cause component of the cause-and-prejudice analysis requires more than a but-for causal relationship between the cause and the default. Lee must also show, given the state of the trial when the motion was made, that an external factor "impeded counsel's efforts to comply with the State's procedural rule." Murray v. Carrier, 477 U.S. 478, 488 (1986). While the departure of his key witnesses may have taken him by surprise (and caused him not to comply with Rule 24.09's writing requirement), nothing about their quick exit stopped him from making a complete oral motion and explaining their absence, the substance of their anticipated testimony, and its materiality.

Nor has Lee shown that an evidentiary hearing is needed to determine whether "a constitutional violation has probably resulted in the conviction of one who is actually innocent." Id., at 496. To fall within this "narrow class of cases," McCleskey v. Zant, 499 U.S. 467, 494 (1991), Lee must demonstrate "that it is more likely than not that no reasonable juror would have convicted him in light of the new evidence." Schlup v. Delo, supra, at 332. Lee would offer the testimony of his mother, stepfather, and sister; but to this day, almost eight years after the trial, Lee has not produced a shred of tangible evidence corroborating their story that he had flown to California to attend a 4–month long birthday party at the time of the murder. To acquit, the jury would have to overlook this problem, ignore the relatives' motive to concoct an alibi for their kin, and discount the prosecution's four eyewitnesses. Even with the relatives' testimony, a reasonable juror could vote to convict.

* * *

"Flying banners of federalism, the Court's opinion actually raises storm signals of a most disquieting nature." So wrote Justice Harlan, dissenting in Henry v. Mississippi, 379 U.S., at 457. The disruption he predicted failed to spread, not because *Henry's* approach was sound but because in later cases the Court, heeding his admonition, refrained from following the course *Henry* prescribed. Though the Court disclaims reliance upon *Henry,* it has in fact revived that case's discredited rationale. Serious doubt is now cast upon many state procedural rules and the convictions sustained under them.

Sound principles of federalism counsel against this result. I would affirm the judgment of the Court of Appeals.

SECTION 10.   EFFECT OF A PRIOR STATE JUDGMENT

Page 551. Add to Footnote 127.

It took three years for the Ninth Circuit to decide, on remand, that the preclusive effect of the Delaware judgment at issue in the principal case was binding on the Epstein plaintiffs. In an opinion reported in 1997 at 126 F.3d 1235 but withdrawn in 1999, a divided panel of the Ninth Circuit initially held that the Supreme Court had left it open for the Epstein plaintiffs to challenge the adequacy of the representation of their interests. In 1998 the panel voted to rehear the case. Upon rehearing, one judge having retired and another changing his vote, a divided panel ultimately held that the Supreme Court's decision in the principal case had foreclosed further inquiry into the adequacy of representation of absent class members in the Delaware class action. Epstein v. MCA, Inc., 179 F.3d 641 (9th Cir.1999), cert. denied sub nom. Epstein v. Matsushita Electric Industrial Co., Ltd., 528 U.S. 1004 (1999).

CHAPTER IX

THE LAW APPLIED IN THE FEDERAL COURTS

SECTION 1. THE ERIE DOCTRINE

Page 601. Insert before Salvina Regina College v. Russell

Semtek International Incorporated v. Lockheed Martin Corporation

Supreme Court of the United States, 2001.
531 U.S. 497, 121 S.Ct. 1021, 149 L.Ed.2d 32.

■ JUSTICE SCALIA delivered the opinion of the Court.

This case presents the question whether the claim-preclusive effect of a federal judgment dismissing a diversity action on statute-of-limitations grounds is determined by the law of the State in which the federal court sits.

I

Petitioner filed a complaint against respondent in California state court, alleging breach of contract and various business torts. Respondent removed the case to the United States District Court for the Central District of California on the basis of diversity of citizenship, see 28 U.S.C. §§ 1332, 1441, and successfully moved to dismiss petitioner's claims as barred by California's 2–year statute of limitations. In its order of dismissal, the District Court, adopting language suggested by respondent, dismissed petitioner's claims "in [their] entirety on the merits and with prejudice." Without contesting the District Court's designation of its dismissal as "on the merits," petitioner appealed to the Court of Appeals for the Ninth Circuit, which affirmed the District Court's order. 168 F.3d 501 (1999) (table). Petitioner also brought suit against respondent in the State Circuit Court for Baltimore City, Maryland, alleging the same causes of action, which were not time barred under Maryland's 3–year statute of limitations. Respondent sought injunctive relief against this action from the California federal court under the All Writs Act, 28 U.S.C. § 1651, and removed the action to the United States District Court for the District of Maryland on federal-question grounds (diversity grounds were not available because Lockheed "is a Maryland citizen," Semtek Int'l Inc. v. Lockheed

Martin Corp., 988 F.Supp. 913, 914 (1997)). The California federal court denied the relief requested, and the Maryland federal court remanded the case to state court because the federal question arose only by way of defense. Following a hearing, the Maryland state court granted respondent's motion to dismiss on the ground of res judicata. Petitioner then returned to the California federal court and the Ninth Circuit, unsuccessfully moving both courts to amend the former's earlier order so as to indicate that the dismissal was not "on the merits." Petitioner also appealed the Maryland trial court's order of dismissal to the Maryland Court of Special Appeals. The Court of Special Appeals affirmed, holding that, regardless of whether California would have accorded claim-preclusive effect to a statute-of-limitations dismissal by one of its own courts, the dismissal by the California federal court barred the complaint filed in Maryland, since the res judicata effect of federal diversity judgments is prescribed by federal law, under which the earlier dismissal was on the merits and claim preclusive. 128 Md.App. 39, 736 A.2d 1104 (1999). After the Maryland Court of Appeals declined to review the case, we granted certiorari.

II

Petitioner contends that the outcome of this case is controlled by Dupasseur v. Rochereau, 21 Wall. [88 U.S.] 130, 135, 22 L.Ed. 588 (1875), which held that the res judicata effect of a federal diversity judgment "is such as would belong to judgments of the State courts rendered under similar circumstances," and may not be accorded any "higher sanctity or effect." Since, petitioner argues, the dismissal of an action on statute-of-limitations grounds by a California state court would not be claim preclusive, it follows that the similar dismissal of this diversity action by the California federal court cannot be claim preclusive. While we agree that this would be the result demanded by *Dupasseur*, the case is not dispositive because it was decided under the Conformity Act of 1872, 17 Stat. 196, which required federal courts to apply the procedural law of the forum State in nonequity cases. That arguably affected the outcome of the case. See *Dupasseur*, supra, at 135. See also Restatement (Second) of Judgments § 87, Comment a, p. 315 (1980) (hereinafter Restatement) ("Since procedural law largely determines the matters that may be adjudicated in an action, state law had to be considered in ascertaining the effect of a federal judgment").

Respondent, for its part, contends that the outcome of this case is controlled by Federal Rule of Civil Procedure 41(b), which provides as follows:

"Involuntary Dismissal: Effect Thereof. For failure of the plaintiff to prosecute or to comply with these rules or any order of court, a defendant may move for dismissal of an action or of any claim against the defendant. Unless the court in its order for dismissal otherwise specifies, a dismissal under this subdivision and any dismissal not provided for in this rule, other than a dismissal for lack of jurisdiction, for improper venue, or for failure to join a party under Rule 19, operates as an adjudication upon the merits."

Since the dismissal here did not "otherwise specif[y]" (indeed, it specifically stated that it *was* "on the merits"), and did not pertain to the excepted subjects of jurisdiction, venue, or joinder, it follows, respondent contends, that the dismissal "is entitled to claim preclusive effect." Brief for Respondent 3–4.

Implicit in this reasoning is the unstated minor premise that all judgments denominated "on the merits" are entitled to claim-preclusive effect. That premise is not necessarily valid. The original connotation of an "on the merits" adjudication is one that actually "pass[es] directly on the substance of [a particular] claim" before the court. Restatement § 19, Comment a, at 161. That connotation remains common to every jurisdiction of which we are aware. See ibid. ("The prototyp[ical] [judgment on the merits is] one in which the merits of [a party's] claim are in fact adjudicated [for or] against the [party] after trial of the substantive issues"). And it is, we think, the meaning intended in those many statements to the effect that a judgment "on the merits" triggers the doctrine of res judicata or claim preclusion. See, e.g., Parklane Hosiery Co. v. Shore, 439 U.S. 322, 326, n. 5 (1979) ("Under the doctrine of res judicata, a judgment on the merits in a prior suit bars a second suit involving the same parties or their privies based on the same cause of action"); Goddard v. Security Title Ins. & Guarantee Co., 14 Cal.2d 47, 51, 92 P.2d 804, 806 (1939) ("[A] final judgment, rendered upon the merits by a court having jurisdiction of the cause . . . is a complete bar to a new suit between [the parties or their privies] on the same cause of action" (internal quotation marks and citations omitted)).

But over the years the meaning of the term "judgment on the merits" "has gradually undergone change," R. Marcus, M. Redish, & E. Sherman, Civil Procedure: A Modern Approach 1140–1141 (3d ed.2000), and it has come to be applied to some judgments (such as the one involved here) that do *not* pass upon the substantive merits of a claim and hence do *not* (in many jurisdictions) entail claim-preclusive effect. Compare, e.g., Western Coal & Mining Co. v. Jones, 27 Cal.2d 819, 826, 167 P.2d 719, 724 (1946), and Koch v. Rodlin Enterprises, Inc., 223 Cal.App.3d 1591, 1596, 273 Cal.Rptr. 438, 441 (1990), with Plaut v. Spendthrift Farm, Inc., 514 U.S. 211, 228 (1995) (statute of limitations); *Goddard*, supra, at 50–51, 92 P.2d, at 806–807, and Allston v. Incorporated Village of Rockville Centre, 25 App.Div.2d 545, 546, 267 N.Y.S.2d 564, 565–566 (1966), with Federated Department Stores, Inc. v. Moitie, 452 U.S. 394, 399, n. 3 (1981) (demurrer or failure to state a claim). See also Restatement § 19, Comment *a* and Reporter's Note; 18 C. Wright, A. Miller, & E. Cooper, Federal Practice and Procedure § 4439, pp. 355–358 (1981) (hereinafter Wright & Miller). That

111

is why the Restatement of Judgments has abandoned the use of the term—
"because of its possibly misleading connotations," Restatement § 19, Comment a, at 161.

In short, it is no longer true that a judgment "on the merits" is necessarily a judgment entitled to claim-preclusive effect; and there are a number of reasons for believing that the phrase "adjudication upon the merits" does not bear that meaning in Rule 41(b). To begin with, Rule 41(b) sets forth nothing more than a default rule for determining the import of a dismissal (a dismissal is "upon the merits," with the three stated exceptions, unless the court "otherwise specifies"). This would be a highly peculiar context in which to announce a federally prescribed rule on the complex question of claim preclusion, saying in effect, "All federal dismissals (with three specified exceptions) preclude suit elsewhere, unless the court otherwise specifies."

And even apart from the purely default character of Rule 41(b), it would be peculiar to find a rule governing the effect that must be accorded federal judgments by other courts ensconced in rules governing the internal procedures of the rendering court itself. Indeed, such a rule would arguably violate the jurisdictional limitation of the Rules Enabling Act: that the Rules "shall not abridge, enlarge or modify any substantive right," 28 U.S.C. § 2072(b). Cf. Ortiz v. Fibreboard Corp., 527 U.S. 815, 842 (1999) (adopting a "limiting construction" of Federal Rule of Civil Procedure 23(b)(1)(B) in order to "minimiz[e] potential conflict with the Rules Enabling Act, and [to] avoi[d] serious constitutional concerns"). In the present case, for example, if California law left petitioner free to sue on this claim in Maryland even after the California statute of limitations had expired, the federal court's extinguishment of that right (through Rule 41(b)'s mandated claim-preclusive effect of its judgment) would seem to violate this limitation.

Moreover, as so interpreted, the Rule would in many cases violate the federalism principle of Erie R. Co. v. Tompkins, 304 U.S. 64, 78–80 (1938), by engendering " 'substantial' variations [in outcomes] between state and federal litigation" which would "[l]ikely ... influence the choice of a forum," Hanna v. Plumer, 380 U.S. 460, 467–468 (1965). See also Guaranty Trust Co. v. York, 326 U.S. 99, 108–110 (1945). Cf. Walker v. Armco Steel Corp., 446 U.S. 740, 748–753 (1980). With regard to the claim-preclusion issue involved in the present case, for example, the traditional rule is that expiration of the applicable statute of limitations merely bars the remedy and does not extinguish the substantive right, so that dismissal on that ground does not have claim-preclusive effect in other jurisdictions with longer, unexpired limitation periods. See Restatement (Second) of Conflict of Laws §§ 142(2), 143 (1969); Restatement of Judgments § 49, Comment a (1942). Out-of-state defendants sued on stale claims in California and in other States adhering to this traditional rule would systematically remove state-law suits brought against them to federal court—where, unless otherwise specified, a statute-of-limitations dismissal would bar suit everywhere.

Finally, if Rule 41(b) did mean what respondent suggests, we would surely have relied upon it in our cases recognizing the claim-preclusive effect of federal judgments in federal-question cases. Yet for over half a century since the promulgation of Rule 41(b), we have not once done so. See, e.g., Heck v. Humphrey, 512 U.S. 477, 488–489, n. 9 (1994); Federated Department Stores, Inc. v. Moitie, supra, at 398; Blonder-Tongue Laboratories, Inc. v. University of Ill. Foundation, 402 U.S. 313, 324, n. 12 (1971).

We think the key to a more reasonable interpretation of the meaning of "operates as an adjudication upon the merits" in Rule 41(b) is to be found in Rule 41(a), which, in discussing the effect of voluntary dismissal by the plaintiff, makes clear that an "adjudication upon the merits" is the opposite of a "dismissal without prejudice":

> "Unless otherwise stated in the notice of dismissal or stipulation, the dismissal is without prejudice, except that a notice of dismissal operates as an adjudication upon the merits when filed by a plaintiff who has once dismissed in any court of the United States or of any state an action based on or including the same claim."

See also 18 Wright & Miller, § 4435, at 329, n. 4 ("Both parts of Rule 41 . . . use the phrase 'without prejudice' as a contrast to adjudication on the merits"); 9 *id.*, § 2373, at 396, n. 4 (" '[W]ith prejudice' is an acceptable form of shorthand for 'an adjudication upon the merits' "). See also *Goddard*, 14 Cal.2d, at 54, 92 P.2d, at 808 (stating that a dismissal "with prejudice" evinces "[t]he intention of the court to make [the dismissal] on the merits"). The primary meaning of "dismissal without prejudice," we think, is dismissal without barring the defendant from returning later, to the same court, with the same underlying claim. That will also ordinarily (though not always) have the consequence of not barring the claim from *other* courts, but its primary meaning relates to the dismissing court itself. Thus, Black's Law Dictionary (7th ed.1999) defines "dismissed without prejudice" as "removed from the court's docket in such a way that the plaintiff may refile the same suit on the same claim," id., at 482, 92 P.2d 804, and defines "dismissal without prejudice" as "[a] dismissal that does not bar the plaintiff from refiling the lawsuit within the applicable limitations period," ibid.

We think, then, that the effect of the "adjudication upon the merits" default provision of Rule 41(b)—and, presumably, of the explicit order in the present case that used the language of that default provision—is simply that, unlike a dismissal "without prejudice," the dismissal in the present case barred refiling of the same claim in the United States District Court for the Central District of California. That is undoubtedly a necessary condition, but it is not a sufficient one, for claim-preclusive effect in other

113

courts.[1]

III

Having concluded that the claim-preclusive effect, in Maryland, of this California federal diversity judgment is dictated neither by Dupasseur v. Rochereau, as petitioner contends, nor by Rule 41(b), as respondent contends, we turn to consideration of what determines the issue. Neither the Full Faith and Credit Clause, U.S. Const., Art. IV, § 1,[2] nor the full faith and credit statute, 28 U.S.C. § 1738,[3] addresses the question. By their terms they govern the effects to be given only to state-court judgments (and, in the case of the statute, to judgments by courts of territories and possessions). And no other federal textual provision, neither of the Constitution nor of any statute, addresses the claim-preclusive effect of a judgment in a federal diversity action.

It is also true, however, that no federal textual provision addresses the claim-preclusive effect of a federal-court judgment in a federal-question case, yet we have long held that States cannot give those judgments merely whatever effect they would give their own judgments, but must accord them the effect that this Court prescribes. See Stoll v. Gottlieb, 305 U.S. 165, 171–172 (1938); Gunter v. Atlantic Coast Line R. Co., 200 U.S. 273, 290–291 (1906); Deposit Bank v. Frankfort, 191 U.S. 499, 514–515 (1903). The reasoning of that line of cases suggests, moreover, that even when States are allowed to give federal judgments (notably, judgments in diversity cases) no more than the effect accorded to state judgments, that disposition is by direction of *this* Court, which has the last word on the claim-preclusive effect of *all* federal judgments:

"It is true that for some purposes and within certain limits it is only required that the judgments of the courts of the United States shall be given the same force and effect as are given the judgments of the courts of the States wherein they are rendered; but it is equally true

1. We do not decide whether, in a diversity case, a federal court's "dismissal upon the merits" (in the sense we have described), under circumstances where a state court would decree only a "dismissal without prejudice," abridges a "substantive right" and thus exceeds the authorization of the Rules Enabling Act. We think the situation will present itself more rarely than would the arguable violation of the Act that would ensue from interpreting Rule 41(b) as a rule of claim preclusion; and if it is a violation, can be more easily dealt with on direct appeal.

2. Article IV, § 1 provides as follows:

"Full Faith and Credit shall be given in each State to the public Acts, Records, and judi-cial Proceedings of every other State. And the Congress may by general Laws pre-scribe the Manner in which such Acts, Records and Proceedings shall be proved, and the Effect thereof."

3. Title 28 U.S.C. § 1738 provides in relevant part as follows:

"The records and judicial proceedings of any court of any ... State, Territory or Posses-sion ... shall have the same full faith and credit in every court within the United States and its Territories and Possessions as they have by law or usage in the courts of such State, Territory or Possession from which they are taken."

that whether a Federal judgment has been given due force and effect in the state court is a Federal question reviewable by this court, which will determine for itself whether such judgment has been given due weight or otherwise. . . .

"When is the state court obliged to give to Federal judgments only the force and effect it gives to state court judgments within its own jurisdiction? Such cases are distinctly pointed out in the opinion of Mr. Justice Bradley in *Dupasseur v. Rochereau* [which stated that the case was a diversity case, applying state law under state procedure]." *Deposit Bank,* 191 U.S., at 514–515.

In other words, in *Dupasseur* the State was allowed (indeed, required) to give a federal diversity judgment no more effect than it would accord one of its own judgments only because reference to state law was *the federal rule that this Court deemed appropriate*. In short, federal common law governs the claim-preclusive effect of a dismissal by a federal court sitting in diversity. See generally R. Fallon, D. Meltzer, & D. Shapiro, Hart and Wechsler's The Federal Courts and the Federal System 1473 (4th ed.1996); Degnan, Federalized Res Judicata, 85 Yale L.J. 741 (1976).

It is left to us, then, to determine the appropriate federal rule. And despite the sea change that has occurred in the background law since *Dupasseur* was decided—not only repeal of the Conformity Act but also the watershed decision of this Court in *Erie*—we think the result decreed by *Dupasseur* continues to be correct for diversity cases. Since state, rather than federal, substantive law is at issue there is no need for a uniform federal rule. And indeed, nationwide uniformity in the substance of the matter is better served by having the same claim-preclusive rule (the state rule) apply whether the dismissal has been ordered by a state or a federal court. This is, it seems to us, a classic case for adopting, as the federally prescribed rule of decision, the law that would be applied by state courts in the State in which the federal diversity court sits. See Gasperini v. Center for Humanities, Inc., 518 U.S. 415, 429–431 (1996); Walker v. Armco Steel Corp., 446 U.S., at 752–753; Bernhardt v. Polygraphic Co. of America, 350 U.S. 198, 202–205 (1956); Palmer v. Hoffman, 318 U.S. 109, 117 (1943); Klaxon Co. v. Stentor Elec. Mfg. Co., 313 U.S. 487, 496 (1941); Cities Service Oil Co. v. Dunlap, 308 U.S. 208, 212 (1939). As we have alluded to above, any other rule would produce the sort of "forum-shopping . . . and . . . inequitable administration of the laws" that *Erie* seeks to avoid, *Hanna,* 380 U.S., at 468, since filing in, or removing to, federal court would be encouraged by the divergent effects that the litigants would anticipate from likely grounds of dismissal. See Guaranty Trust Co. v. York, 326 U.S., at 109–110.

This federal reference to state law will not obtain, of course, in situations in which the state law is incompatible with federal interests. If, for example, state law did not accord claim-preclusive effect to dismissals for willful violation of discovery orders, federal courts' interest in the integrity of their own processes might justify a contrary federal rule. No such conflict with potential federal interests exists in the present case. Dismissal of this state cause of action was decreed by the California federal court only because the California statute of limitations so required; and there is no conceivable federal interest in giving that time bar more effect in other courts than the California courts themselves would impose.

* * *

Because the claim-preclusive effect of the California federal court's dismissal "upon the merits" of petitioner's action on statute-of-limitations grounds is governed by a federal rule that in turn incorporates California's law of claim preclusion (the content of which we do not pass upon today), the Maryland Court of Special Appeals erred in holding that the dismissal necessarily precluded the bringing of this action in the Maryland courts. The judgment is reversed, and the case remanded for further proceedings not inconsistent with this opinion.

It is so ordered.

SECTION 2.　FEDERAL COMMON LAW AND IMPLIED RIGHTS OF ACTION

Page 627. Add to Footnote 65

Jeffries, The Right–Remedy Gap in Constitutional Law, 109 Yale L.J. 87 (1999), discusses the legal status of implied remedies. The complicated prerequisites for a Bivens claim asserting a denial of access to courts are discussed in Christopher v. Harbury, 536 U.S. __, 122 S.Ct. 2179 (2002). In Gonzaga University v. Doe, 536 U.S. __, 122 S.Ct. 2268 (2002), also discussed below in connection with p. 638, n. 70, a narrowly divided Court substantially elided issues of implied rights and implied remedies, holding that the question whether a particular federal statute creates a private federal right enforceable against public entities un-der 42 U.S.C. § 1983 requires essentially the same analysis as the more general question whether the statute was intended to create a private right of action against parties not acting under color of state law. In Barnes v. Gorman, 536 U.S. __, 122 S.Ct. 2097 (2002), the Court held that the implied right of action created by Title VI of the Civil Rights Act of 1964 does not extend to punitive damages because such damages are incompatible with the essentially contractual duties imposed by Congress when it attaches conditions to the receipt of federal funds under statutes enacted under its Spending Clause power.

Page 638. Add to Footnote 70

In Gonzaga University v. Doe, 536 U.S. __, 122 S.Ct. 2268 (2002), also discussed above in connection with p. 627, n. 65, a narrowly divided Court limited the scope of the private remedy conferred by 42 U.S.C. § 1983 to cases in which a predicate federal right was unambiguously conferred on the party seeking relief under § 1983. A § 1983 plaintiff may not rely merely on a showing that the defendant violated a federal duty that in some more general sense benefits the plaintiff or serves the interests of the plaintiff. Thus the breach of a federal duty to maintain the confidentiality of student records imposed on a private university as a condition of receiving federal funds was held not to be actionable under § 1983—notwithstanding the assumption that by making unauthorized disclosures to state officials the university was acting under color of state law—because federal law did

not unambiguously confer on the plaintiff student an individualized federal right to have his personal information remain confidential.

Page 638. Insert after Thompson v. Thompson

Correctional Services Corporation v. Malesko

Supreme Court of the United States, 2001.
534 U.S. 61, 122 S.Ct. 515, 151 L.Ed.2d 456.

■ CHIEF JUSTICE REHNQUIST delivered the opinion of the Court.

We decide here whether the implied damages action first recognized in Bivens v. Six Unknown Fed. Narcotics Agents, 403 U.S. 388 (1971), should be extended to allow recovery against a private corporation operating a halfway house under contract with the Bureau of Prisons. We decline to so extend *Bivens.*

Petitioner Correctional Services Corporation (CSC), under contract with the federal Bureau of Prisons (BOP), operates Community Corrections Centers and other facilities that house federal prisoners and detainees.[38] Since the late 1980's, CSC has operated Le Marquis Community Correctional Center (Le Marquis), a halfway house located in New York City. Respondent John E. Malesko is a former federal inmate who, having been convicted of federal securities fraud in December 1992, was sentenced to a term of 18 months' imprisonment under the supervision of the BOP. During his imprisonment, respondent was diagnosed with a heart condition and treated with prescription medication. Respondent's condition limited his ability to engage in physical activity, such as climbing stairs.

In February 1993, the BOP transferred respondent to Le Marquis where he was to serve the remainder of his sentence. Respondent was assigned to living quarters on the fifth floor. On or about March 1, 1994, petitioner instituted a policy at Le Marquis requiring inmates residing below the sixth floor to use the staircase rather than the elevator to travel from the first-floor lobby to their rooms. There is no dispute that respondent was exempted from this policy on account of his heart condition. Respondent alleges that on March 28, 1994, however, Jorge Urena, an employee of petitioner, forbade him to use the elevator to reach his fifth-

---

38. Petitioner is hardly unique in this regard. The BOP has since 1981 relied exclusively on contracts with private institutions and state and local governments for the operation of halfway house facilities to help federal prisoners reintegrate into society. The BOP contracts not only with for-profit entities like petitioner, but also with charitable organizations like Volunteers for America (which operates facilities in Indiana, Louisiana, Maryland, Minnesota, New York, and Texas), the Salvation Army (Arkansas, Florida, Illinois, North Carolina, Tennessee, and Texas), Progress House Association (Oregon), Triangle Center (Illinois), and Catholic Social Services (Pennsylvania).

117

floor bedroom. Respondent protested that he was specially permitted elevator access, but Urena was adamant. Respondent then climbed the stairs, suffered a heart attack, and fell, injuring his left ear.

Three years after this incident occurred, respondent filed a pro se action against CSC and unnamed CSC employees in the United States District Court for the Southern District of New York. Two years later, now acting with counsel, respondent filed an amended complaint which named Urena as 1 of the 10 John Doe defendants. The amended complaint alleged that CSC, Urena, and unnamed defendants were "negligent in failing to obtain requisite medication for [respondent's] condition and were further negligent by refusing [respondent] the use of the elevator." App. 12. It further alleged that respondent injured his left ear and aggravated a pre-existing condition "[a]s a result of the negligence of the Defendants." Ibid. Respondent demanded judgment in the sum of $1 million in compensatory damages, $3 million in anticipated future damages, and punitive damages "for such sum as the Court and/or [j]ury may determine." Id., at 13.

The District Court treated the amended complaint as raising claims under Bivens v. Six Unknown Fed. Narcotics Agents, supra, and dismissed respondent's cause of action in its entirety. Relying on our decision in FDIC v. Meyer, 510 U.S. 471 (1994), the District Court reasoned that "a *Bivens* action may only be maintained against an individual," and thus was not available against petitioner, a corporate entity. App. to Pet. for Cert. 20a. With respect to Urena and the unnamed individual defendants, the complaint was dismissed on statute of limitations grounds.

The Court of Appeals for the Second Circuit affirmed in part, reversed in part, and remanded. 229 F.3d 374 (C.A.2 2000). That court affirmed dismissal of respondent's claims against individual defendants as barred by the statute of limitations. Respondent has not challenged that ruling, and the parties agree that the question whether a *Bivens* action might lie against a private individual is not presented here. With respect to petitioner, the Court of Appeals remarked that *Meyer* expressly declined " 'to expand the category of defendants against whom *Bivens*-type actions may be brought to include not only federal agents, but federal agencies as well.' " 229 F.3d, at 378 (quoting *Meyer*, supra, at 484, 114 S.Ct. 996 (emphasis deleted)). But the court reasoned that private entities like petitioner should be held liable under *Bivens* to "accomplish the ... important *Bivens* goal of providing a remedy for constitutional violations." 229 F.3d, at 380.

We granted certiorari, 532 U.S. 902 (2001), and now reverse.[39]

39. The Courts of Appeals have divided on whether FDIC v. Meyer, 510 U.S. 471 (1994), forecloses the extension of *Bivens* to private entities. Compare Hammons v. Norfolk Southern Corp., 156 F.3d 701, 705 (C.A.6 1998) ("Nothing in *Meyer* prohibits a *Bivens* claim against a private corporation that engages in federal action"), with Kauffman v. Anglo–American School of Sofia, 28 F.3d 1223, 1227 (C.A.D.C.1994)

118

In Bivens v. Six Unknown Fed. Narcotics Agents, 403 U.S. 388 (1971), we recognized for the first time an implied private action for damages against federal officers alleged to have violated a citizen's constitutional rights. Respondent now asks that we extend this limited holding to confer a right of action for damages against private entities acting under color of federal law. He contends that the Court must recognize a federal remedy at law wherever there has been an alleged constitutional deprivation, no matter that the victim of the alleged deprivation might have alternative remedies elsewhere, and that the proposed remedy would not significantly deter the principal wrongdoer, an individual private employee. We have heretofore refused to imply new substantive liabilities under such circumstances, and we decline to do so here.

Our authority to imply a new constitutional tort, not expressly authorized by statute, is anchored in our general jurisdiction to decide all cases "arising under the Constitution, laws, or treaties of the United States." 28 U.S.C. § 1331. See, e.g., Schweiker v. Chilicky, 487 U.S. 412, 420–421 (1988); Bush v. Lucas, 462 U.S. 367, 373–374 (1983). We first exercised this authority in *Bivens,* where we held that a victim of a Fourth Amendment violation by federal officers may bring suit for money damages against the officers in federal court. *Bivens* acknowledged that Congress had never provided for a private right of action against federal officers, and that "the Fourth Amendment does not in so many words provide for its enforcement by award of money damages for the consequences of its violation." 403 U.S., at 396. Nonetheless, relying largely on earlier decisions implying private damages actions into federal statutes, see id., at 397 (citing J.I. Case Co. v. Borak, 377 U.S. 426, 433 (1964)); 403 U.S., at 402–403, n. 4 (Harlan, J., concurring in judgment) ("The *Borak* case is an especially clear example of the exercise of federal judicial power to accord damages as an appropriate remedy in the absence of any express statutory authorization of a federal cause of action"), and finding "no special factors counseling hesitation in the absence of affirmative action by Congress," id., at 395–396, we found an implied damages remedy available under the Fourth Amendment.[40]

In the decade following *Bivens,* we recognized an implied damages remedy under the Due Process Clause of the Fifth Amendment, Davis v.

("[Under] *Meyer's* conclusion that public federal agencies are not subject to *Bivens* liability, it follows that equivalent private entities should not be liable either"). We hold today that it does.

40. Since our decision in *Borak,* we have retreated from our previous willingness to imply a cause of action where Congress has not provided one. See, e.g., Central Bank of Denver, N.A. v. First Interstate Bank of Denver, N. A., 511 U.S. 164, 188 (1994); Transamerica Mortgage Advisors, Inc. v.

Lewis, 444 U.S. 11, 15–16 (1979); Cannon v. University of Chicago, 441 U.S. 677, 688 (1979); id., at 717–718 (REHNQUIST, J., concurring). Just last Term it was noted that we "abandoned" the view of *Borak* decades ago, and have repeatedly declined to "revert" to "the understanding of private causes of action that held sway 40 years ago." Alexander v. Sandoval, 532 U.S. 275, 287 (2001).

Passman, 442 U.S. 228 (1979), and the Cruel and Unusual Punishment Clause of the Eighth Amendment, Carlson v. Green, 446 U.S. 14 (1980). In both *Davis* and *Carlson,* we applied the core holding of *Bivens,* recognizing in limited circumstances a claim for money damages against federal officers who abuse their constitutional authority. In *Davis,* we inferred a new right of action chiefly because the plaintiff lacked any other remedy for the alleged constitutional deprivation. 442 U.S., at 245 ("For Davis, as for Bivens, it is damages or nothing"). In *Carlson,* we inferred a right of action against individual prison officials where the plaintiff's only alternative was a Federal Tort Claims Act (FTCA) claim against the United States. 446 U.S., at 18–23. We reasoned that the threat of suit against the United States was insufficient to deter the unconstitutional acts of individuals. Id., at 21 ("Because the *Bivens* remedy is recoverable against individuals, it is a more effective deterrent than the FTCA remedy"). We also found it "crystal clear" that Congress intended the FTCA and *Bivens* to serve as "parallel" and "complementary" sources of liability. 446 U.S., at 19–20.

Since *Carlson* we have consistently refused to extend *Bivens* liability to any new context or new category of defendants. In Bush v. Lucas, supra, we declined to create a *Bivens* remedy against individual Government officials for a First Amendment violation arising in the context of federal employment. Although the plaintiff had no opportunity to fully remedy the constitutional violation, we held that administrative review mechanisms crafted by Congress provided meaningful redress and thereby foreclosed the need to fashion a new, judicially crafted cause of action. 462 U.S., at 378, n. 14. We further recognized Congress' institutional competence in crafting appropriate relief for aggrieved federal employees as a "special factor counseling hesitation in the creation of a new remedy." Id., at 380. See also id., at 389 (noting that "Congress is in a far better position than a court to evaluate the impact of a new species of litigation between federal employees"). We have reached a similar result in the military context, Chappell v. Wallace, 462 U.S. 296, 304 (1983), even where the defendants were alleged to have been civilian personnel, United States v. Stanley, 483 U.S. 669 (1987).

In Schweiker v. Chilicky, we declined to infer a damages action against individual government employees alleged to have violated due process in their handling of Social Security applications. We observed that our "decisions have responded cautiously to suggestions that *Bivens* remedies be extended into new contexts." 487 U.S., at 421. In light of these decisions, we noted that "[t]he absence of statutory relief for a constitutional violation ... does not by any means necessarily imply that courts should award money damages against the officers responsible for the violation." Id., at 421–422. We therefore rejected the claim that a *Bivens* remedy should be implied simply for want of any other means for challenging a constitutional deprivation in federal court. It did not matter, for example, that "[t]he creation of a *Bivens* remedy would obviously offer the prospect of relief for injuries that must now go unredressed." 487 U.S., at 425. See also *Bush,*

120

supra, at 388 (noting that "existing remedies do not provide complete relief for the plaintiff"); *Stanley,* supra, at 683. ("[I]t is irrelevant to a special factors analysis whether the laws currently on the books afford Stanley . . . an adequate federal remedy for his injuries" (internal quotation marks omitted)). So long as the plaintiff had an avenue for some redress, bedrock principles of separation of powers foreclosed judicial imposition of a new substantive liability. *Chilicky*, supra, at 425–427.

Most recently, in *FDIC v. Meyer,* we unanimously declined an invitation to extend *Bivens* to permit suit against a federal agency, even though the agency—because Congress had waived sovereign immunity—was otherwise amenable to suit. 510 U.S., at 484–486. Our opinion emphasized that "the purpose of *Bivens* is to deter *the officer*," not the agency. Id., at 485 (emphasis in original) (citing Carlson v. Green, supra, at 21). We reasoned that if given the choice, plaintiffs would sue a federal agency instead of an individual who could assert qualified immunity as an affirmative defense. To the extent aggrieved parties had less incentive to bring a damages claim against individuals, "the deterrent effects of the *Bivens* remedy would be lost." 510 U.S., at 485 .. Accordingly, to allow a *Bivens* claim against federal agencies "would mean the evisceration of the Bivens remedy, rather than its extension." 510 U.S., at 485. We noted further that "special factors" counseled hesitation in light of the "potentially enormous financial burden" that agency liability would entail. Id., at 486.

From this discussion, it is clear that the claim urged by respondent is fundamentally different from anything recognized in *Bivens* or subsequent cases. In 30 years of *Bivens* jurisprudence we have extended its holding only twice, to provide an otherwise nonexistent cause of action against *individual officers* alleged to have acted unconstitutionally, or to provide a cause of action for a plaintiff who lacked *any alternative remedy* for harms caused by an individual officer's unconstitutional conduct. Where such circumstances are not present, we have consistently rejected invitations to extend *Bivens,* often for reasons that foreclose its extension here.[41]

The purpose of *Bivens* is to deter individual federal officers from committing constitutional violations. *Meyer* made clear that the threat of litigation and liability will adequately deter federal officers for *Bivens* purposes no matter that they may enjoy qualified immunity, 510 U.S., at 474, 485, are indemnified by the employing agency or entity, id., at 486, or are acting pursuant to an entity's policy, id., at 473–474. *Meyer* also made clear that the threat of suit against an individual's employer was not the kind of deterrence contemplated by *Bivens*. See 510 U.S., at 485 ("If we were to imply a damages action directly against federal agencies . . . there

---

41. JUSTICE STEVENS' claim that this case does not implicate an "extension" of *Bivens*, post, at [125, 128] (dissenting opinion), might come as some surprise to the Court of Appeals which twice characterized its own holding as "extending *Bivens* liability to reach private corporations." 229 F.3d 374, 381 (C.A.2 2000). See also ibid. ("*Bivens* liability should extend to private corporations").

would be no reason for aggrieved parties to bring damages actions against individual officers. [T]he deterrent effects of the *Bivens* remedy would be lost"). This case is, in every meaningful sense, the same. For if a corporate defendant is available for suit, claimants will focus their collection efforts on it, and not the individual directly responsible for the alleged injury. See, e.g., TXO Production Corp. v. Alliance Resources Corp., 509 U.S. 443, 464 (1993) (plurality opinion) (recognizing that corporations fare much worse before juries than do individuals); id., at 490–492 (O'CONNOR, J., dissenting) (same) (citing authorities). On the logic of *Meyer,* inferring a constitutional tort remedy against a private entity like CSC is therefore foreclosed.

Respondent claims that even under *Meyer's* deterrence rationale, implying a suit against private corporations acting under color of federal law is still necessary to advance the core deterrence purpose of *Bivens.* He argues that because corporations respond to market pressures and make decisions without regard to constitutional obligations, requiring payment for the constitutional harms they commit is the best way to discourage future harms. That may be so, but it has no relevance to *Bivens,* which is concerned solely with deterring the unconstitutional acts of individual officers. If deterring the conduct of a policy-making entity was the purpose of *Bivens,* then *Meyer* would have implied a damages remedy against the Federal Deposit Insurance Corporation; it was after all an agency policy that led to *Meyer's* constitutional deprivation. *Meyer,* supra, at 473–474. But *Bivens* from its inception has been based not on that premise, but on the deterrence of individual officers who commit unconstitutional acts.

There is no reason for us to consider extending *Bivens* beyond this core premise here.[42] To begin with, *no federal prisoners* enjoy respondent's contemplated remedy. If a federal prisoner in a BOP facility alleges a constitutional deprivation, he may bring a *Bivens* claim against the offending individual officer, subject to the defense of qualified immunity. The prisoner may not bring a *Bivens* claim against the officer's employer, the United States or the BOP. With respect to the alleged constitutional

42. JUSTICE STEVENS claims that our holding in favor of petitioner portends "tragic consequence[s]," post, at [128], and "jeopardize[s] the constitutional rights of ... tens of thousands of inmates," post, at [128]. He refers to examples of cases suggesting that private correctional providers routinely abuse and take advantage of inmates under their control. Post, at [128], n. [47] (citing Brief for Legal Aid Society of New York as Amicus Curiae 8–25). See also Brief for American Civil Liberties Union as Amicus Curiae 14–16, and n. 6 (citing and discussing "abundant" examples of such abuse). In all but one of these examples, however, the private facility in question housed *state* prisoners—prisoners who already enjoy a right of action against private correctional providers under 42 U.S.C. § 1983. If it is true that the imperatives for deterring the unconstitutional conduct of private correctional providers are so strong as to demand that we imply a new right of action directly from the Constitution, then abuses of authority should be *less* prevalent in state facilities, where Congress already provides for such liability. That the trend appears to be just the opposite is not surprising given the BOP's oversight and monitoring of its private contract facilities, see Brief for United States as Amicus Curiae 4–5, 24–26, which JUSTICE STEVENS does not mention.

deprivation, his only remedy lies against the individual; a remedy *Meyer* found sufficient, and which respondent did not timely pursue. Whether it makes sense to impose asymmetrical liability costs on private prison facilities alone is a question for Congress, not us, to decide.

Nor are we confronted with a situation in which claimants in respondent's shoes lack effective remedies. Cf. *Bivens,* 403 U.S., at 410 (Harlan, J., concurring in judgment) ("For people in Bivens' shoes, it is damages or nothing"); *Davis,* 442 U.S., at 245 ("For Davis, as for Bivens, it is damages or nothing" (internal quotation marks omitted)). It was conceded at oral argument that alternative remedies are at least as great, and in many respects greater, than anything that could be had under *Bivens.* Tr. of Oral Arg. 41–42, 43. For example, federal prisoners in private facilities enjoy a parallel tort remedy that is unavailable to prisoners housed in government facilities. See Brief in Opposition 13. This case demonstrates as much, since respondent's complaint in the District Court arguably alleged no more than a quintessential claim of negligence. It maintained that named and unnamed defendants were "*negligent* in failing to obtain requisite medication . . . and were further *negligent* by refusing . . . use of the elevator." App. 12 (emphasis added). It further maintained that respondent suffered injuries "[a]s a result of the *negligence* of the Defendants." Ibid. (emphasis added). The District Court, however, construed the complaint as raising a *Bivens* claim, presumably under the Cruel and Unusual Punishment Clause of the Eighth Amendment. Respondent accepted this theory of liability, and he has never sought relief on any other ground. This is somewhat ironic, because the heightened "deliberate indifference" standard of Eighth Amendment liability, Estelle v. Gamble, 429 U.S. 97, 104 (1976), would make it considerably more difficult for respondent to prevail than on a theory of ordinary negligence, see, e.g., Farmer v. Brennan, 511 U.S. 825, 835 (1994) ("[D]eliberate indifference describes a state of mind more blameworthy than negligence").

This also makes respondent's situation altogether different from *Bivens,* in which we found alternative state tort remedies to be "inconsistent or even hostile" to a remedy inferred from the Fourth Amendment. 403 U.S., at 393–394. When a federal officer appears at the door and requests entry, one cannot always be expected to resist. See id., at 394 ("[A] claim of authority to enter is likely to unlock the door"). Yet lack of resistance alone might foreclose a cause of action in trespass or privacy. Ibid. Therefore, we reasoned in *Bivens* that other than an implied constitutional tort remedy, "there remain[ed] . . . but the alternative of resistance, which may amount to a crime." Id., at 395 (internal quotation marks and citation omitted). Such logic does not apply to respondent, whose claim of negligence or deliberate indifference requires no resistance to official action, and whose lack of alternative tort remedies was due solely to strategic choice.[43]

---

43. Where the government has directed a contractor to do the very thing that is the subject of the claim, we have recognized this as a special circumstance where the

Inmates in respondent's position also have full access to remedial mechanisms established by the BOP, including suits in federal court for injunctive relief and grievances filed through the BOP's Administrative Remedy Program (ARP). See 28 CFR § 542.10 (2001) (explaining ARP as providing "a process through which inmates may seek formal review of an issue which relates to any aspect of their confinement"). This program provides yet another means through which allegedly unconstitutional actions and policies can be brought to the attention of the BOP and prevented from recurring. And unlike the *Bivens* remedy, which we have never considered a proper vehicle for altering an entity's policy, injunctive relief has long been recognized as the proper means for preventing entities from acting unconstitutionally.

In sum, respondent is not a plaintiff in search of a remedy as in *Bivens* and *Davis.* Nor does he seek a cause of action against an individual officer, otherwise lacking, as in *Carlson.* Respondent instead seeks a marked extension of *Bivens,* to contexts that would not advance *Bivens'* core purpose of deterring individual officers from engaging in unconstitutional wrongdoing. The caution toward extending *Bivens* remedies into any new context, a caution consistently and repeatedly recognized for three decades, forecloses such an extension here.

The judgment of the Court of Appeals is reversed.

It is so ordered.

■ JUSTICE SCALIA, with whom JUSTICE THOMAS joins, concurring.

I join the opinion of the Court because I agree that a narrow interpretation of the rationale of Bivens v. Six Unknown Fed. Narcotics Agents, 403 U.S. 388 (1971), would not logically produce its application to the circumstances of this case. The dissent is doubtless correct that a broad interpretation of its rationale *would* logically produce such application, but I am not inclined (and the Court has not been inclined) to construe *Bivens* broadly.

In joining the Court's opinion, however, I do not mean to imply that, *if* the narrowest rationale of *Bivens did* apply to a new context, I *would* extend its holding. I would not. *Bivens* is a relic of the heady days in which this Court assumed common-law powers to create causes of action— decreeing them to be "implied" by the mere existence of a statutory or constitutional prohibition. As the Court points out, ante, at [119], and n. [40], we have abandoned that power to invent "implications" in the statutory field, see Alexander v. Sandoval, 532 U.S. 275, 287 (2001). There is even greater reason to abandon it in the constitutional field, since an "implication" imagined in the Constitution can presumably not even be repudiated by Congress. I would limit *Bivens* and its two follow-on cases

contractor may assert a defense. Boyle v. United Technologies Corp., 487 U.S. 500 (1988). The record here would provide no basis for such a defense.

(Davis v. Passman, 442 U.S. 228 (1979), and Carlson v. Green, 446 U.S. 14 (1980)) to the precise circumstances that they involved.

■ JUSTICE STEVENS, with whom JUSTICE SOUTER, JUSTICE GINSBURG, and JUSTICE BREYER join, dissenting.

In Bivens v. Six Unknown Fed. Narcotics Agents, 403 U.S. 388 (1971), the Court affirmatively answered the question that it had reserved in Bell v. Hood, 327 U.S. 678 (1946): whether a violation of the Fourth Amendment "by *a federal agent* acting under color of his authority gives rise to a cause of action for damages consequent upon his unconstitutional conduct." 403 U.S., at 389 (emphasis added). Nearly a decade later, in Carlson v. Green, 446 U.S. 14 (1980), we held that a violation of the Eighth Amendment by federal prison officials gave rise to a *Bivens* remedy despite the fact that the plaintiffs also had a remedy against the United States under the Federal Tort Claims Act (FTCA). We stated: *"Bivens* established that the victims of a constitutional violation by *a federal agent* have a right to recover damages against the official in federal court despite the absence of any statute conferring such a right." 446 U.S., at 18 (emphasis added).

In subsequent cases, we have decided that a *Bivens* remedy is not available for every conceivable constitutional violation. We have never, however, qualified our holding that Eighth Amendment violations are actionable under *Bivens*.... Nor have we ever suggested that a category of federal agents can commit Eighth Amendment violations with impunity.

The parties before us have assumed that respondent's complaint has alleged a violation of the Eighth Amendment. The violation was committed by a federal agent—a private corporation employed by the Bureau of Prisons to perform functions that would otherwise be performed by individual employees of the Federal Government. Thus, the question presented by this case is whether the Court should create an exception to the straightforward application of *Bivens* and *Carlson,* not whether it should extend our cases beyond their "core premise," ante, at [122]. This point is evident from the fact that prior to our recent decision in FDIC v. Meyer, 510 U.S. 471 (1994), the Courts of Appeals had consistently and correctly held that corporate agents performing federal functions, like human agents doing so, were proper defendants in *Bivens* actions.

Meyer, which concluded that federal agencies are not suable under *Bivens,* does not lead to the outcome reached by the Court today. In that case, we did not discuss private corporate agents, nor suggest that such agents should be viewed differently from human ones. Rather, in *Meyer,* we drew a distinction between "federal agents" and "an agency of the Federal Government," 510 U.S., at 473. Indeed, our repeated references to the Federal Deposit Insurance Corporation's (FDIC) status as a "federal agency" emphasized the FDIC's affinity to the federal sovereign. We expressed concern that damages sought directly from federal agencies, such as the FDIC, would "creat[e] a potentially enormous financial burden for the Federal Government." Id., at 486. And it must be kept in mind that *Meyer* involved the FDIC's waiver of sovereign immunity, which, had the Court in *Meyer* recognized a cause of action, would have permitted the very sort of lawsuit that *Bivens* presumed impossible: "a direct action against the Government." 510 U.S., at 485.

Moreover, in *Meyer,* as in Bush v. Lucas, 462 U.S. 367 (1983), and Schweiker v. Chilicky, 487 U.S. 412 (1988), we were not dealing with a well-recognized cause of action. The cause of action alleged in *Meyer* was a violation of procedural due process, and as the *Meyer* Court noted, "a *Bivens* action alleging a violation of the Due Process Clause of the Fifth Amendment may be appropriate in some contexts, but not in others." 510 U.S., at 484, n. 9. Not only is substantive liability assumed in the present case, but respondent's Eighth Amendment claim falls in the heartland of substantive *Bivens* claims.[44]

Because *Meyer* does not dispose of this case, the Court claims that the rationales underlying *Bivens*—namely, lack of alternative remedies and deterrence—are not present in cases in which suit is brought against a private corporation serving as a federal agent. However, common sense, buttressed by all of the reasons that supported the holding in *Bivens,* leads to the conclusion that corporate agents should not be treated more favorably than human agents.

First, the Court argues that respondent enjoys alternative remedies against the corporate agent that distinguish this case from *Bivens.* In doing so, the Court characterizes *Bivens* and its progeny as cases in which plaintiffs lacked *"any alternative remedy,"* ante, at [121]. In *Bivens,* however, even though the plaintiff's suit against the Federal Government under state tort law may have been barred by sovereign immunity, a suit against the officer himself under state tort law was theoretically possible. Moreover, as the Court recognized in *Carlson, Bivens* plaintiffs also have remedies available under the FTCA. Thus, the Court is incorrect to portray *Bivens* plaintiffs as lacking any other avenue of relief, and to imply as a result that respondent in this case had a substantially wider array of non-*Bivens* remedies at his disposal than do other *Bivens* plaintiffs.[45] If alterna-

---

44. The Court incorrectly assumes that we are being asked "to imply a new constitutional tort," ante, at [119]. The tort here is, however, well established; the only question is whether a remedy in damages is available against a limited class of tortfeasors.

45. The Court recognizes that the question whether a *Bivens* action would lie against the individual employees of a private corporation like Correctional Services Corporation (CSC) is not raised in the present case. Ante, at [118]. Both petitioner and respondent have assumed *Bivens* would apply to

these individuals, and the United States as amicus maintains that such liability would be appropriate under *Bivens*. It does seem puzzling that *Bivens* liability would attach to the private individual employees of such corporations—*subagents* of the Federal Government—but not to the corporate agents themselves. However, the United States explicitly maintains this to be the case, and the reasoning of the Court's opinion relies, at least in part, on the availability of a remedy against employees of private prisons. Cf. ante, at [123] (noting that *Meyer* "found sufficient" a remedy against the

tive remedies provide a sufficient justification for closing the federal forum here, where the defendant is a private corporation, the claims against the individual defendants in *Carlson*, in light of the FTCA alternative, should have been rejected as well.

It is ironic that the Court relies so heavily for its holding on this assumption that alternative effective remedies—primarily negligence actions in state court—are available to respondent. See ante, at 123–124]. Like Justice Harlan, I think it "entirely proper that these injuries be compensable according to uniform rules of federal law, especially in light of the very large element of federal law which must in any event control the scope of official defenses to liability." *Bivens*, 403 U.S., at 409 (opinion concurring in judgment). And aside from undermining uniformity, the Court's reliance on state tort law will jeopardize the protection of the full scope of federal constitutional rights. State law might have comparable causes of action for tort claims like the Eighth Amendment violation alleged here, see ante, at [123], but other unconstitutional actions by prison employees, such as violations of the Equal Protection or Due Process Clauses, may find no parallel causes of action in state tort law. Even though respondent here may have been able to sue for some degree of relief under state law because his Eighth Amendment claim could have been pleaded as negligence, future plaintiffs with constitutional claims less like traditional torts will not necessarily be so situated.[46]

Second, the Court claims that the deterrence goals of *Bivens* would not be served by permitting liability here. Ante, at [121] (citing *Meyer*). It cannot be seriously maintained, however, that tort remedies against corporate employers have less deterrent value than actions against their employees. As the Court has previously noted, the "organizational structure" of private prisons "is one subject to the ordinary competitive pressures that normally help private firms adjust their behavior in response to the incentives that tort suits provide—pressures not necessarily present in government departments." Richardson v. McKnight, 521 U.S. 399, 412

individual officer, "*which respondent did not timely pursue*"(emphasis added)).

46. The Court blames respondent, who filed his initial complaint pro se, for the lack of state remedies in this case; according to the Court, respondent's failure to bring a negligence suit in state court was "due solely to strategic choice," ante, at 522. Such strategic behavior, generally speaking, is imaginable, but there is no basis in the case before us to charge respondent with acting strategically. Cf. ibid. (discussing how proving a federal constitutional claim would be "considerably more difficult" than proving a state negligence claim). Respondent filed his complaint in federal court because he

believed himself to have been severely maltreated while in federal custody, and he had no legal counsel to advise him to do otherwise. Without the aid of counsel, respondent not only failed to file for state relief, but he also failed to name the particular prison guard who was responsible for his injuries, resulting in the eventual dismissal of the claims against the individual officers as time barred. Respondent may have been an unsophisticated plaintiff, or, at worst, not entirely diligent about determining the identify of the guards, but it can hardly be said that "strategic choice" was the driving force behind respondent's litigation behavior.

(1997). Thus, the private corporate entity at issue here is readily distinguishable from the federal agency in *Meyer*. Indeed, a tragic consequence of today's decision is the clear incentive it gives to corporate managers of privately operated custodial institutions to adopt cost-saving policies that jeopardize the constitutional rights of the tens of thousands of inmates in their custody.[47]

The Court raises a concern with imposing "asymmetrical liability costs on private prison facilities," ante, at [123], and further claims that because federal prisoners in Government-run institutions can only sue officers, it would be unfair to permit federal prisoners in private institutions to sue an "officer's employer," ibid. Permitting liability in the present case, however, would *produce* symmetry: both private and public prisoners would be unable to sue the principal (i.e., the Government), but would be able to sue the primary federal agent (i.e., the government official or the corporation). Indeed, it is the *Court's* decision that creates asymmetry—between federal and state prisoners housed in private correctional facilities. Under 42 U.S.C. § 1983, a state prisoner may sue a private prison for deprivation of constitutional rights, see Lugar v. Edmondson Oil Co., 457 U.S. 922, 936–937 (1982) (permitting suit under § 1983 against private corporations exercising "state action"), yet the Court denies such a remedy to that prisoner's federal counterpart. It is true that we have never expressly held that the contours of *Bivens* and § 1983 are identical. The Court, however, has recognized sound jurisprudential reasons for parallelism, as different standards for claims against state and federal actors "would be incongruous and confusing." Butz v. Economou, 438 U.S. 478, 499 (1978) (internal quotation marks omitted); cf. Bolling v. Sharpe, 347 U.S. 497, 500 (1954) ("In view of our decision that the Constitution prohibits the states from maintaining racially segregated public schools, it would be unthinkable that the same Constitution would impose a lesser duty on the Federal Government"). The value of such parallelism was in fact furthered by *Meyer,* since § 1983 would not have provided the plaintiff a remedy had he pressed a similar claim against a state agency.

It is apparent from the Court's critical discussion of the thoughtful opinions of Justice Harlan and his contemporaries, ante, at [119], and n. [40], and from its erroneous statement of the question presented by this case as whether *Bivens* "should be extended" to allow recovery against a private corporation employed as a federal agent, ante, at [117], that the driving force behind the Court's decision is a disagreement with the holding in *Bivens* itself.[48] There are at least two reasons why it is improper for the

---

47. As amici for respondent explain, private prisons are exempt from much of the oversight and public accountability faced by the Bureau of Prisons, a federal entity. See, e.g., Brief for Legal Aid Society of New York as Amicus Curiae 8–25. Indeed, because a private prison corporation's first loyalty is to its stockholders, rather than the public interest, it is no surprise that cost-cutting measures jeopardizing prisoners' rights are more likely in private facilities than in public ones.

48. See also ante, at [124] (Scalia, J., concurring) (arguing that *Bivens* is a "relic of

Court to allow its decision in this case to be influenced by that predisposition. First, as is clear from the legislative materials cited in *Carlson*, 446 U.S., at 19–20, see also ante, at [120], Congress has effectively ratified the *Bivens* remedy; surely Congress has never sought to abolish it. Second, a rule that has been such a well-recognized part of our law for over 30 years should be accorded full respect by the Members of this Court, whether or not they would have endorsed that rule when it was first announced. For our primary duty is to apply and enforce settled law, not to revise that law to accord with our own notions of sound policy.

    I respectfully dissent.

Page 639. Add at end of Comment

    For a comprehensive review of the past four decades of Supreme Court decisions dealing with Indian law, see Frickey, A Common Law for Our Age of Colonialism: The Judicial Divestiture of Indian Tribal Authority over Nonmembers, 109 Yale L.J. 1 (1999). Nicholas, American–Style Justice in No Man's Land, 36 Ga.L.Rev. 895 (2002), discusses an array of problems encountered in applying basic constitutional and statutory doctrines of federal jurisdiction to parties and transactions connected to tribes and tribal land.

... heady days" and should be limited, along with Carlson v. Green, 446 U.S. 14 (1980), and Davis v. Passman, 442 U.S. 228 (1979), to its facts). Such hostility to the core of *Bivens* is not new. See, e.g., Carlson, 446 U.S., at 32 (REHNQUIST, J., dissenting) ("[T]o dispose of this case as if *Bivens* were rightly decided would in the words of Mr. Justice Frankfurter be to start with an 'unreality' "). Nor is there anything new in the Court's disregard for precedent concerning well-established causes of action. See Alexander v. Sandoval, 532 U.S. 275, 294–297 (2001) (STEVENS, J., dissenting).

CHAPTER X

PROCEDURE IN THE DISTRICT COURT

SECTION 1. PROCESS

Page 640. Add to Footnote 1

The scope of the personal jurisdiction that may be obtained by service of process under Civil Rule 4(k)(2) is comprehensively discussed in United States v. Swiss American Bank, Ltd., 191 F.3d 30 (1st Cir.1999).

Page 653. Add to Footnote 11

The right to object to personal jurisdiction may be "forfeited" by dilatory conduct in moving to dismiss the complaint for lack of personal jurisdiction, notwithstanding that this defense was properly asserted in the answer to the complaint and thus was not "waived" under Civil Rule 12(h)(1)(B). See Hamilton v. Atlas Turner, Inc., 197 F.3d 58, 62–63 (2d Cir.1999), where a three-year delay in moving to dismiss the complaint was deemed so egregious that the appellate court concluded "not only that Atlas forfeited its personal jurisdiction defense, but also that this is the rare case where a district judge's contrary ruling exceeds the bounds of allowable discretion."

Page 687. Add to Footnote 40

See Gardner, Comment, An Attempt to Intervene in the Confusion: Standing Requirements for Rule 24 Intervenors, 69 U.Chi. L.Rev. 681 (2002).

SECTION 2. JOINDER OF PARTIES AND CLAIMS

E. CLASS ACTIONS

Page 703. Add to Footnote 45

For commentary on Amchem and related issues, see Issacharoff, Governance and Legitimacy in the Law of Class Actions, 1999 Sup.Ct.Rev. 187; Rubenstein, A Transactional Model of Litigation, 89 Geo.L.J. 371 (2001), Weber, A Consent–Based Approach to Class Action Settlement: Improving Amchem Products, Inc. v. Windsor, 59 Ohio St.L.J. 1155 (1998); Willging, Mass Torts Problems and Proposals: A Report to the Mass Torts Working Group, 187 F.R.D. 328 (1999).

The Private Securities Litigation Reform Act of 1995 (PSLRA) imposes a "gauntlet" of procedural restrictions on the prosecution of a securities-law class action. The Securities Litigation Uniform Standards Act of 1998 contains an exceptionally broad removal provision permitting securities-law class actions to be removed from state courts to the federal courts, where they become subject to the restrictive provisions of PSLRA. See Branson, Securities Litigation in State Courts—Something Old, Something New, Something Borrowed . . ., 76 Wash.Univ. L.Q. 509 (1998); Branson, Running the Gauntlet, A Description of the Arduous, and Now Often Fatal, Journey for Plaintiffs in Federal Securities Law Actions, 65 U.Cinn.L.Rev. 3 (1996); Branson, Chasing the Rogue Professional After the Private Securities Litigation Reform Act of 1995, 50 SMU L.Rev. 91 (1996).

The discretionary power of the courts of appeals to hear interlocutory appeals from class-certification rulings under new Rule 23(f) is discussed and applied in Blair v. Equifax Check Services, Inc., 181 F.3d 832 (7th Cir.1999). See also Solimine & Hines, Deciding to Decide: Class Action Certification and Interlocutory Review by the Unit-ed States Courts of Appeals under Rule 23(f), 41 Wm. & Mary L.Rev. 1531 (2000). In Rutstein v. Avis Rent-A-Car Systems, 211 F.3d 1228 (11th Cir.2000), noted 114 Harv. L. Rev. 1793 (2001), it was held that Rule 23(f) gave an appellate court the authority to review and reverse a trial court's grant of class certification based on the appellate court's de novo review of the facts relating to the predominance issue under Rule 23(b)(3).

A nonnamed member of Rule 23(b)(1) class action who has entered a timely objection to the settlement of the class action at the fairness hearing in the district court need not intervene in the action in order to appeal the district court's approval of the settlement. Devlin v. Scardelletti, 536 U.S. ___, 122 S.Ct. 2005 (2002), also discussed below in connection with p. 748, n. 1.

CHAPTER XI

APPELLATE JURISDICTION AND PROCEDURE

SECTION 1. THE COURTS OF APPEALS

Page 748. Add to Footnote 1

In Devlin v. Scardelletti, 536 U.S. __, 122 S.Ct. 2005 (2002), also discussed above in connection with p. 703, n. 45, the Court held that a nonnamed member of a Rule 23(b)(1) class, who entered a timely but unsuccessful objection to the fairness of a proposed settlement of the class action, has the right under 28 U.S.C. § 1291 to appeal the approval of the settlement. Justice O'Connor wrote for a divided Court that "[t]he label 'party' does not indicate an absolute characteristic, but rather a conclusion about the applicability of various procedures that may differ based on context." 536 U.S. at __, 122 S.Ct. at 2011. Justice Scalia dissented, joined by Justices Kennedy and Thomas. The dissenters would have preferred maintaining a bright-line test for party status by requiring the objecting nonnamed class member formally to intervene in order to have the right to appeal. The entire Court evidently agreed that a nonnamed class member who had lodged a timely but unsuccessful objection to a personally binding settlement, would be entitled to intervene as of right under Federal Rule of Civil Procedure 24(a) in order to gain unquestioned "party" status for purposes of appeal. But the majority refused to tie the right to appeal to intervenor status, deeming a requirement of prior intervention to be an unnecessary complication in tension with the "statutory basis" under § 1291 of "the right to appeal from an action that finally disposes of one's rights." 536 U.S. at __, 122 S.Ct. at 2013.

Page 750. Add to Footnote 3

In Holmes Group, Inc. v. Vornado Air Circulation Systems, Inc., 535 U.S. __, 122 S.Ct. 1889 (2002), also discussed above in connection with p. 109, n. 11a, and p. 222, n. 16, the Court extended the well-pleaded complaint rule to hold that the Federal Circuit lacks appellate jurisdiction of a case in which the defendant asserts a patent-infringement claim as a compulsory counterclaim. Under 28 U.S.C. § 1295(a)(1), the Federal Circuit's appellate jurisdiction is defined in terms of cases in which the district court's jurisdiction "was based, in whole or in part, on section 1338 ...," with further qualifications that restrict the Federal Circuit's jurisdiction to patent rather copyright, mask-work, and trademark cases. In Christianson v. Colt Industries Operating Corp., 486 U.S. 800, 808 (1988), the Court had held that the same test determines whether a case "arises under" the patent laws for purposes of § 1338 as applies under the general federal-question statute, § 1331. Resolving a surprisingly open question under its general "arising under" jurisprudence, the Court extended the core principle of the well-pleaded complaint rule—that statutory "arising under" jurisdiction cannot be based on a federal defense—to also foreclose "arising under" based on any federal issue presented in the answer as opposed to the complaint. Since a counterclaim is asserted in the answer, a patent-infringement counterclaim does not confer § 1338 jurisdiction on the district court, and hence cannot make a case otherwise within the jurisdiction of the district court into one

that is within the appellate jurisdiction of the Federal Circuit.

Page 761. Add to Footnote 8

In Cunningham v. Hamilton County, Ohio, 527 U.S. 198 (1999), the collateral order doctrine was held inapplicable to permit interlocutory review of an order imposing

sanctions on an attorney even though the attorney no longer represented any party in the continuing litigation.

Page 770. Add to Footnote 11

Interlocutory appeal of orders determining whether an action may proceed as a class action is specially authorized by Civil Rule 23(f), reprinted at p. 663 of the main volume and discussed in the main volume at p. 703, n. 45, and p. 751, n. 4.

Difficult issues of appealability arise in connection with the Federal Arbitration Act, which permits interlocutory appeal of an order denying arbitration but requires a "final decision" before an order compelling arbitration is appealable. This has led many circuits to classify arbitration proceedings as either "independent" or "embedded." The first category involves litigation in which the only issue is the duty to arbitrate. An order compelling arbitration leaves nothing left to be determined by the district court, and is therefore immediately appealable. The second category involves litigation that includes a claim that arbitration should be compelled along with other non-arbitral claims. An order compelling arbitration in an embedded proceeding is

generally held not subject to immediate appeal. The district court will stay litigation of the non-arbitral claims pending arbitration, so there is no final decision as required by both 28 U.S.C. § 1291 and 9 U.S.C. § 16(a)(3). A circuit split has arisen at the margins of this doctrine. Most circuits hold flatly that orders compelling arbitration in embedded proceedings are not appealable, but this overlooks the finality of a such an order when it is accompanied by a dismissal on the merits of all other claims. In such circumstances, a well-reasoned opinion of the Eleventh Circuit has upheld its appellate jurisdiction to review an order compelling arbitration in an embedded case. Randolph v. Green Tree Financial Corp.—Alabama, 178 F.3d 1149 (11th Cir.1999). The Sixth and Tenth Circuits agree with the Eleventh, but the First, Fifth, Seventh, Eighth, and Ninth Circuits continue flatly to prohibit appeal from any order compelling arbitration in an embedded proceeding.

Page 775. Add to Footnote 16

It was held in Hill v. Henderson, 195 F.3d 671 (D.C.Cir.1999), that a district court's order dismissing one count of a complaint was not rendered a "final decision" appealable under 28 U.S.C. § 1291 by virtue of the court's transfer of the remaining counts to another district. Absent certification of the dismissal order for immediate

appeal pursuant to Rule 54(b), appeal of the dismissal order must await the transferee court's resolution of the other counts, and must then be appealed in the transferee circuit. The circuits are divided, however. See McGeorge v. Continental Airlines, 871 F.2d 952 (10th Cir.1989), which the District of Columbia Circuit expressly declined to follow.

†